AMERICAN BLUE

Elizabeth Alexander is a leading American poet whose work has been inspired by a wide range of influence, from history, literature, art and music, dreams and stories to the rich infinity of the African American experience. She is president of the Mellon Foundation, the US's largest funder in the arts, culture, and humanities. In January 2009 she read the inaugural poem for the swearing-in of President Barack Obama, 'Praise Song for the Day'. Born in Harlem, New York City, she grew up in Washington, DC. She is also an essayist, playwright, teacher and scholar of African-American literature and culture, and has given readings and lectures on African American literature and culture in many countries.

Her most recent book, *The Trayvon Generation* (2022), is a galvanising meditation on the power of art and culture to illuminate America's unresolved problem with race and the challenges facing young Black America. Among the fifteen books she has written or co-authored, her poetry collection *American Sublime* was a finalist for the Pulitzer Prize in Poetry in 2006, and her memoir, *The Light of the World*, was a finalist for the Pulitzer Prize in Biography and the National Book Critics Circle Award in 2015. Her other books include *Crave Radiance: New and Selected Poems 1990–2010* (2010), *Power and Possibility: Essays, Reviews, Interviews* (2007) and *The Black Interior: Essays* (2004). Her first UK publication, *American Blue: Selected Poems* (Bloodaxe Books, 2006), drew on her first four collections: *The Venus Hottentot* (1990), *Body of Life* (1996), *Antebellum Dream Book* (2001) and *American Sublime* (2005).

Elizabeth Alexander has held distinguished professorships at Smith College, Columbia University, and Yale University, where she taught for fifteen years and chaired the African American Studies Department. She has been awarded the Jackson Poetry Prize, the John Simon Guggenheim Memorial Foundation Fellowship, the George Kent Award, and the National Endowment for the Arts Fellowship.

ELIZABETH
ALEXANDER

AMERICAN BLUE

SELECTED POEMS

BLOODAXE BOOKS

ISBN: 978 1 85224 730 0

First published 2006 by
Bloodaxe Books Ltd,
Eastburn,
South Park,
Hexham,
Northumberland NE46 1BS.

www.bloodaxebooks.com
For further information about Bloodaxe titles
please visit our website and join our mailing list
or write to the above address for a catalogue.

Digital reprint of the 2006 Bloodaxe Books edition.

CONTENTS

FROM **Antebellum Dream Book** (2001)

FROM **Body of Life** (1996)

ACKNOWLEDGEMENTS

This first UK edition of Elizabeth Alexander's work is drawn from her first four US collections, *Venus Hottentot* (University Press of Virginia, 1990; Graywolf Press, 2004), *Body of Life* (Tia Chucha Press, Chicago, 1996), *Antebellum Dream Book* (Graywolf Press, 2001) and *American Sublime* (Graywolf Press, 2005), and from her book of essays, *The Black Interior* (Graywolf Press, 2004).

from

AMERICAN SUBLIME

(2005)

Little Slave Narrative #1: Master

He would order the women to pull up their clothes
'in Alabama style', as he called it. He would whip them

for not complying. He taught bloodhounds
to chase down negro boys, hence the expression

'hell-hounds on my trail'. He was fond of peach brandy,
put ads in the paper: *Search high, search low*

for my runaway Isaac, my runaway Joe,
his right cheek scarred, occasioned by buckshot,

runaway Ben Fox, very black, chunky made,
two hundred dollars live, and if dead,

bring his dead body, so I may look at it.

Ellipsis

White-blossoming trees
in front of the house

in Sparta, Georgia,
where they together lived:

free woman of color
(black, white, Cherokee),

white male slaver,
and their children,

who slept with the mother
in a mouse room connected

to his rooms through secret doors.
He gave his daughters diamonds

which they wore set in rings
on their toes, and hid in their hair.

Distant white relatives
fought for the railroad stock

when he died, and they won.
They also got the house.

You can smell the funk
of the haints in the walls:

mildew, semen, camphor,
oft-handled bills, coin metal,

cornbread breath that whispers
and swallows and breathes.

One day, as in the best
bodice-rippers, the house

burned down to the ground,
burnt down by the distant white cousin

who no doubt heard the ghosts
humming and fussing, rattling,

ratcheting, singing. Burn!
she screamed. So it did.

The fussing quieted. In its place,
wind in the willows, a whiff of

something sweet, something sour,
something always in its place.

Smile

When I see a black man smiling
like that, nodding and smiling
with both hands visible, mouthing

'Yes, Officer', across the street,
I think of my father, who taught us
the words 'cooperate', 'officer',

to memorise badge numbers,
who has seen black men shot at
from behind in the warm months north.

And I think of the fine line –
hairline, eyelash, fingernail paring –
the whisper that separates

obsequious from *safe*. Armstrong,
Johnson, Robinson, Mays.
A woman with a yellow head

of cotton candy hair stumbles out
of a bar at after-lunchtime
clutching a black man's arm as if

for her life. And the brother
smiles, and his eyes are flint
as he watches all sides of the street.

Matrimonio

1 *Blues*

If I am the baby who does not fit
in the overhead compartment, in
the weekender tote, if I am the baby
who will bounce off a lap on the jitney,
who sleeps in a dresser drawer or shoebox,
then I am no rosebud, no foundling, no pearl.
I am outsized, enormous for a baby,
too giant for footie pajamas
(the cradle wood splits, the tree bough breaks),
not baby then but mother, a mama
for whom there is no cupped palm, no bosom,
no cradle, no lap, just the wide world
to be crossed in strides, and the floorboards
to be paced until they wear away to dust.

2 *Oscar de la Renta*

Oscar de la Renta
adores my avoirdupois,
every ounce, every pouf of me.

His voice never raises,
all sentences prefaced
My darling, *My dear*.

He's arranged for his best seamstress
to measure and tuck. In a few
weeks' time, the gown will be ready.

He will escort me into Society.
We'll eat a light dinner
on trays, in the library, before.

How he loves
bacon, lettuce,
and tomato sandwiches!

Even in this field of plenty
(my real life, my marriage),
a cold wind blows sometimes

– raised voices, sharp words –
and in dances Oscar de la Renta
to do the Continental

and each time, I give him my hand.

3 *The Dancers Dressed in White*

It was the dancers dressed in white running
in a line together like spume to the shore
who made me run to where they were, bringing
the baby along in a grocery cart,
distracting him with bananas. There
I made a mistake, soul-kissed the man
who gave me armfuls of dresses, a green dress,
(I never believed I could wear green) kissing
his mouth, making plans to follow him and dance.
Shuck the corn, harvest jig, and I have erred,
but I have not worn white in a century,
not kissed, not danced, not maiden, nor autumn gold
nor spring, nor run full out to the shoreline,
its white edges always receding.

4 *Siesta*

The sounds of the day turned to dust, particles
fizzing in a sunlight shaft, faraway
lawn mowers, leaf-blowers, motorcar motors,

and the purr of each baby in his sleep,
and Papa's snores, and the tick-tock clock –
even Doña on the bed with Papa,

the kitchen floor swept, food set in the cupboard,
hyacinth nipped and in water releasing
its wild musk throughout the quiet house.

Even Doña has taken her shoes off,
lain down on the bed, and fitted the arch
of her foot in her husband's, and slept.

Krishna Denies Eating Mud

Blue boy, the apple
of his mother's ravening eye.

Blue as the noon sky,
Blue as the sea,
Beautiful Krishna
Come to me!

The boy eats rocks, eats nails,
great fistfuls of mud.

Mother pries the bud-mouth open
and looks inside: a globe,

planets, oceans, telescopes,
Milky Way, books,

beasts, flowers, vegetables,
minutes, time, history,

the universe in Krishna's mouth!
Mother faints, astonished.

Krishna: You will remember none of this.

Mother (awakening): *Angel, blue angel,*
Come sit on my lap,
Come sit on my starry skirt.

The Dream That I Told My Mother-in-Law

In the room almost filled with our bed,
the small bedroom, the king-sized bed high up
and on casters so sometimes we would roll,
in the room in the corner of the corner
apartment on top of a hill so the bed would roll,
we felt as if we might break off and drift,
float, and become our own continent.
When your mother first entered our apartment
she went straight to that room and libated our bed
with water from your homeland. Soon she saw
in my cheeks the fire and poppy stain,
and soon thereafter on that bed came the boy.
Then months, then the morning I cracked first one
then two then three eggs in a white bowl
and all had double yolks, and your mother
(now our mother) read the signs. Signs everywhere,
signs rampant, a season of signs and a vial
of white dirt brought across three continents
to the enormous white bed that rolled
and now held three, and soon held four,
four on the bed, two boys, one man, and me,
our mother reading all signs and blessing our bed,
blessing our bed filled with babies, blessing our bed
through her frailty, blessing us and our bed,
blessing us and our bed.
                                        She began to dream
of childhood flowers, her long-gone parents.
I told her my dream in a waiting room:
a photographer photographed women,
said her portraits revealed their truest selves.
She snapped my picture, peeled back the paper,
and there was my son's face, my first son, my self.
Mamma loved that dream so I told it again.

And soon she crossed over to her parents,
sisters, one son (War took that son.
We destroy one another), and women came
by twos and tens wrapped in her same fine white
bearing huge pans of stew, round breads, homemade wines,

and men came in suits with their ravaged faces
and together they cried and cried and cried
and keened and cried and the sound
was a live hive swelling and growing,
all the water in the world, all the salt, all the wails,
and the sound grew too big for the building and finally
lifted what needed to be lifted from the casket and we quieted
and watched it waft up and away like feather, like ash.
Daughter, she said, when her journey began, *You are a mother now,*
and you have to take care of the world.

Notes From

We are Underground. Underground:
a cinder-block barrack, red clay warren,
at times a seaside cottage far away.
Austere and opulent, spartan and lush,
where we struggle to hear ourselves think.
It is not '45, when the A-bomb was dropped
(kimono flowers burned onto skin, shadows
remaindered on walls after bodies disintegrate),
not '55 when Emmett Till was lynched,
nor '63, when the Birmingham church girls
were blown to smithereens (and hear now the sister
who survived, now in her fifties, tell of the dress sash
she was in the midst of tying, of her glass eye
that pops out and rolls across the room),
not '65, when Malcolm, not '68, when King,
when My Lai, not and not and not but now,
which is why we are down in the Underground:

Sun Salutation at dawn, we fill our lungs
with available air and light, exhale
the detritus, breathe in again. How much light
does a bomb flash make, and what can it do?
Can it photostat a body with kimono print?
Today, the Vietnam hero reveals his Bronze Star
was won by ordering civilians shot
as his men escaped the village. The village woman
says she saw her sisters and brothers and mothers
and aunts lined up and shot into a pile. Who
is surprised to hear how war medals are won?
Underground, analysis must overcome surprise.

In Chicago, Girl X who can no longer speak
tells a courtroom in nods and grunts what happened
and who dragged and raped and beat her
out of herself, so she forgot it, until
smoke from a magician's act at school
reminded her of his smell, and the rest.

What reminded the war hero thirty years later
that he ordered a village slaughtered?
His absent leg tells us what we want
war heroes to say. We are Underground
because twelve-year-old boys are sent to prison
for the rest of their lives and eighteen-year-olds
recruited to "guard" them, and dead children

are "collateral damage" to the homegrown bomber
who will sit in the electric chair on television
so a public can watch him blaze out, and find succor.
Too many people have seen too much
and lived to tell, or not tell, or tell
with their silent, patterned bodies,
their glass eyes, gone legs, flower-printed flesh,
ropey scar tissue, nods and grunts, tics and eczemas.
Under, then, under the front porch, in the loam
of the burning and smoking land, the de-
foliated, under that pyre of bones, we scrabble,
and struggle together to hear ourselves think.

The African Picnic

World Cup finals, France v. Brasil.
We gather in Gideon's yard and grill.
The TV sits in the bright sunshine.
We want Brasil but Brasil won't win.
Aden waves a desultory green and yellow flag.
From the East to the West to the West to the East
we scatter and settle and scatter some more.
Through the window, Mamma watches from the cool indoors.

Jonah scarfs meat off of everybody's plate,
kicks a basketball long and hollers, 'goal',
then roars like the mighty lion he is.
Baby is a pasha surrounded by pillows
and a bevy of Horn of Africa girls
who coo like lovers, pronounce his wonders,
oil and massage him, brush his hair.
My African family is having a picnic, here in the USA.

Who is here and who is not?
When will the phone ring from far away?
Who in a few days will say goodbye?
Who will arrive with a package from home?
Who will send presents in other people's luggage
and envelopes of money in other people's pockets?
Other people's children have become our children
here at the African picnic.

In a parking lot, in a taxi-cab,
in a winter coat, in an airport queue,
at the INS, on the telephone,
on the crosstown bus, on a South Side street,
in a brand-new car, in a djellaba,
with a cardboard box, with a Samsonite,
with an airmail post, with a bag of spice,
at the African picnic people come and go.

The mailman sees us say goodbye and waves
with us, goodbye, goodbye, as we throw popcorn,
ululate, ten or twelve suitcases stuffed in the car.

Goodbye, Mamma, goodbye –
The front door shut. The driveway bare.
Goodbye, Mamma, goodbye.
The jet alights into the night,
a huge, metal machine in flight,
Goodbye, Mamma, goodbye.
At the African picnic, people come and go
and say goodbye.

Autumn Passage

On suffering, which is real.
On the mouth that never closes,
the air that dries the mouth.

On the miraculous dying body,
its greens and purples.
On the beauty of hair itself.

On the dazzling toddler:
'Like eggplant,' he says,
when you say 'Vegetable',

'Chrysanthemum' to 'Flower'.
On his grandmother's suffering, larger
than vanished skyscrapers,

September zucchini,
other things too big. For her glory
that goes along with it,

glory of grown children's vigil,
communal fealty, glory
of the body that operates

even as it falls apart, the body
that can no longer even make fever
but nonetheless burns

florid and bright and magnificent
as it dims, as it shrinks,
as it turns to something else.

Ars Poetica #1,002: Rally

I dreamed a pronouncement
about poetry and peace.

'People are violent,'
I said through the megaphone

on the quintessentially
frigid Saturday

to the rabble stretching
all the way up First.

'People do violence
unto each other

and unto the earth
and unto its creatures.

Poetry,' I shouted, 'Poetry,'
I screamed, 'Poetry

changes none of that
by what it says

or how it says, none.
But a poem is a living thing

made by living creatures
(live voice in a small box)

and as life
it is all that can stand

up to violence.'
I put down the megaphone.

The first clap I heard
was my father's,

then another, then more,
wishing for the same thing

in different vestments.
I never thought, why me?

I had spoken a truth
offered up by ancestral dreams

and my father understood
my declaration

as I understood the mighty man
still caught in the vapor

between this world and that
when he said, 'The true intellectual

speaks truth to power.'
If I understand my father

as artist, I am free,
said my friend, of the acts

of her difficult father.
So often it comes down

to the father, his showbiz,
while the mother's hand

shapes us, beckons us
to ethics, slaps our faces

when we err, soothes
the sting, smoothes the earth

we trample daily, in light
and in dreams. Rally

all your strength, rally
what mother and father

together have made:
us on this planet,

erecting, destroying.

Ars Poetica #92: Marcus Garvey on Elocution

Elocution means to speak out.
That is to say, if you have a tale to tell,
tell it and tell it well.

This I was taught.

To speak properly you must have sound and good teeth.
You must have clear nostrils.
Your lungs must be sound.
Never try to make a speech on a hungry stomach.

Don't chew your words but talk them out plainly.
Always see that your clothing is properly arranged before you get on
a platform.
You should not make any mistake in pronouncing your words
because that invites amusement for certain people.

To realise I was trained for this,
expected to speak out, to speak well.
To realise, my family believed
I would have words for others.

An untidy leader is always a failure.
A leader's hair should always be well kept.
His teeth must also be in perfect order.
Your shoes and other garments must also be clean.
If you look ragged, people will not trust you.

My father's shoe-shine box:
black Kiwi, cordovan Kiwi,
the cloths, the lambswool brush.

My grandmother's dressing table:
potions for disciplining
anything scraggle or stray.

For goodness sake, always speak out,
said Marcus Garvey,
said my parents,
said my grandparents,
and meant it.

Ars Poetica #100: I Believe

Poetry, I tell my students,
is idiosyncratic. Poetry

is where we are ourselves
(though Sterling Brown said

'Every "I" is a dramatic "I"'),
digging in the clam flats

for the shell that snaps,
emptying the proverbial pocketbook.

Poetry is what you find
in the dirt in the corner,

overhear on the bus, God
in the details, the only way

to get from here to there.
Poetry (and now my voice is rising)

is not all love, love, love,
and I'm sorry the dog died.

Poetry (here I hear myself loudest)
is the human voice,

and are we not of interest to each other?

AMISTAD

Amistad

After the tunnel of no return
After the roiling Atlantic, the black Atlantic, black and mucilaginous
After skin to skin in the hold and the picked handcuff locks
After the mutiny
After the fight to the death on the ship
After picked handcuff locks and the jump overboard
After the sight of no land and the zigzag course
After the Babel which settles like silt into silence
and silence and silence, and the whack
of lashes and waves on the side of the boat
After the half cup of rice, the half cup of sea-water
the dry swallow and silence
After the sight of no land
After two daughters sold to pay off a father's debt
After Cinque himself a settled debt

After, white gulf between stanzas

the space at the end

the last quatrain

The Blue Whale

swam alongside the vessel for hours.
I saw her breach. The spray when she sounded
soaked me (the lookout) on deck. I was joyous.
There her oily, rainbowed, lingering wake,
ambergris print on the water's sheer skin,
she skimmed and we skimmed and we sped
straight on toward home, on the glorious wind.

Then something told her, Turn (whales travel
in pods and will beach themselves rather than split) –
toward her pod? – and the way she turned was not
our way. I begged and prayed and begged for her
companionship, the guide-light of her print,
North Star (I did imagine) of her spout.
But she had elsewhere to go. I watched
the blue whale's silver spout. It disappeared.

Absence

In the absence of women on board,
when the ship reached the point where no landmass
was visible in any direction
and the funk had begun to accrue –
human funk, spirit funk, soul funk – who
commenced the moaning? Who first hummed that deep
sound from empty bowels, roiling stomachs,
from back of the frantically thumping heart?
In the absence of women, of mothers,
who found the note that would soon be called 'blue',
the first blue note from one bowel, one throat,
joined by dark others in gnarled harmony.
Before the head-rag, the cast-iron skillet,
new blue awaited on the other shore,
invisible, as yet unhummed. Who knew
what note to hit or how? In the middle
of the ocean, in the absence of women,
there is no deeper deep, no bluer blue.

boy haiku

the motherless child
rests his hand on a dead man's
forehead till it cools.

Poro Society

Without leopard skin, leather,
antelope horns, wart-hog tusks,
crocodile jaws, raffia muffs,

without the sacred bush,
the primordial grove,
our ancient initiations,

we must find a way
to teach the young man
on board with us.

We contend
with the forces of evil
in the universe.

Aggressive magic
addresses the need for control
in an imperfect world.

Approach

With shore in sight, the wind dies and we slow.
Up from the water bobs a sleek black head
with enormous dark eyes that question us:

who and what are you? Why? Then another
and another and another of those
faces, till our boat is all surrounded.

The dark creatures are seen to be
seals, New England gray seals, we later learn.
They stare. We stare. Not all are blackest black:

some piebald, some the dull gray of the guns
our captors used to steal and corral us,
some the brown-black of our brothers, mothers,

and two milky blue-eyed albino pups.
Albino: the congenital absence
of normal pigmentation. Something gone

amiss. Anomaly, aberration.

Connecticut

They squint from shore
at scarlet-shirted blackamoors.

The battered boat sails in.
White sky, black sea, black skin,

a low black schooner,
armed black men on deck

in shawls, pantaloons,
a Cuban planter's hat –

parched, starved,
dressed in what they found

in the dry goods barrels,
the Africans squint

at trees not their trees,
at shore not their shore.

Other Cargo

Saddles and bridles,
bolts of ribbon,
calico, muslin, silk,
beans, bread, books,
gloves, raisins, cologne,
olives, mirrors, vermicelli,
parasols, rice, black bombazine.

Education

In 1839, to enter University,
the Yale men already knew Cicero,

Dalzel's *Graeca Minora*, then learned more Latin prosody,
Stiles on astronomy, Dana's mineralogy.

Each year they named a Class Bully
who would butt heads with sailors in town.

'The first foreign heathen ever seen',
Obookiah, arrived from Hawaii in '09.

The most powerful telescope in America
was a recent gift to the school

and through it, they were first to see
the blazing return of Halley's comet.

Ebeneezer Peter Mason
and Hamilton Lanphere Smith

spent all their free time at the instrument
observing the stars, their systems,

their movement and science and magic,
pondering the logic of mysteries that twinkle.

Some forty years before, Banneker's
eclipse-predicting charts and almanacs

had gone to Thomas Jefferson
to prove 'that nature has given our brethren

talents equal to other colors of men'.
Benjamin Banneker, born free,

whose people came from Guinea,
who taught himself at twenty-two (the same age

as the graduates) to carve entirely from wood
a watch which kept exquisite time,

accurate to the blade-sharp second.

The Yale Men

One by one the Yale men come
to teach their tongue to these
caged Africans so they might tell

in court what happened on the ship
and then, like Phillis Wheatley,
find the Yale men's God

and take Him for their own.

Teacher

(Josiah Willard Gibbs)

I learn to count in Mende one to ten,
then hasten to the New York docks to see
if one of these black seamen is their kind.

I run to one and then another, count.
Most look at me as though I am quite mad.
I've learned to count in Mende one to ten!

I shout, exhausted as the long day ends
and still no hope to know the captive's tale.
Is any of these black seamen their kind?

I'd asked an old Congo sailor to come
to the jail, but his tongue was the wrong one,
I learned. To count in Mende one to ten

begin *eta, fili, kian-wa, naeni.*
I spy a robust fellow loading crates.
Is this the black seaman who is their kind?

He stares at me as though I am in need,
but tilts his head and opens up his ear
and counts to me in Mende one to ten,
this one at last, this black seaman, their kind.

Translator

(James Covey)

I was stolen from Mendeland as a child
then rescued by the British ship *Buzzard*
and brought to Freetown, Sierra Leone.

I love ships and the sea, joined this crew
of my own accord, set sail as a teen,
now re-supplying in New York Harbor.

When the white professor first came to me
babbling sounds, I thought he needed help
until *weta*, my mother's six, hooked my ear

and I knew what he was saying, and I knew
what he wanted in an instant, for we had heard
wild tales of black pirates off New London,

the captives, the low black schooner like
so many ships, an infinity of ships fatted
with Africans, men, women, children

as I was. Now it is my turn to rescue.
I have not spoken Mende in some years,
yet every night I dream it, or silence.

To New Haven, to the jail. To my people.
Who am I now? This them, not them. We burst
with joy to speak and settle to the tale:

We killed the cook, who said he would cook us.
They rubbed gunpowder and vinegar in our wounds.
We were taken away in broad daylight.

And in a loud voice loud as a thousand waves
I sing my father's song. It shakes the jail.
I sing from my entire black body.

Physiognomy

> Monday, September 16, 1839
> *Another of the captured Africans named Bulwa (or Woolwah) died on Saturday night. This is the third who has died in this city, and the thirteenth since their leaving Havana. One more remains sick in this city, the others having been removed to Hartford on Saturday, to await their trial on Tuesday the 17th. Several are still affected with the white flux, the disease which has proved fatal to so many of them.*
>
> THE DAILY HERALD, NEW HAVEN

Kimbo, 5 feet 6 inches, with mustaches and long beard,
in middle life, calls himself Manding. Very intelligent,

he counts thus: 1. *eta*, 2. *fili*, 3. *kian-wa*, 4. *naeni*,
5. *loelu*, 6. *weta*, 7. *wafura*, 8. *wayapa*,
9. *ta-u*, 10. *pu*.

Shuma, 5 feet 6 inches, spoke
over the corpse of Tha
after Reverend Mister Bacon's prayer.

Konoma, 5 feet 4 inches, with incisor teeth
pressed outward and filed, with large lips
and projecting mouth, tattooed on the forehead,

calls himself Congo (Congo
of Ashmun's map of Liberia,
or Kanga, or Vater).

They are represented by travelers as handsome.
They are supposed to be more ancient of the soil than Timaris.
Their language, according to Port Chad, is distinct from any other.

Biah, 5 feet 4-1/2 inches with remarkably pleasant countenance,
with hands whitened by scars from gunpowder,
calls himself Duminah (Timari),

counts also in Timari.
He counts in Bullom thus.
He counts in Manding like Kwong.

With face broad in the middle
With sly and mirthful countenance (rather old)
With full Negro features
With hair shorn in rows from behind
With permanent flexion of two fingers on right hand
A mere boy, calls himself Manding
With depression of skull from a forehead wound
Tattooed on breast
With narrow and high head
With large head and high cheekbones
Marked on face by the smallpox
Stout and fleshy

Teme, 4 feet 3 inches, a young girl,
calls herself Congo but when further interrogated
says her parents were Congo, she a Manding.

Observe that in this examination
no one when asked for his name
gave any other than an African name.

No one when asked
to count counted in any
language other than African.

There was no appearance in any of them,
so far as I could judge,
of having been from Africa more than two or three months.

Constitutional

Mary Barber's children beg their mother
to take them into town each day to see
the Africans on the New Haven Green
let out of their cells for movement and air.

A New York shilling apiece to the jailer
who tucks away coins in a full suede purse.
The children push through skirts, past waistcoats,
to see the Africans turn somersets.

In the open air, in the bright sunlight,
the Africans chatter, and sound to
the children like blackbirds or cawing gulls.
The Africans spring. The Africans do not smile.

Mende Vocabulary

they
my father
our father
your father
my mother
our mother
my book
his house
one ship
two men
all men
good man
bad man
white man
black man

I eat
he eats
we eat
they sleep
I see God
did I say it right?
we sleep
I make
he makes
they have eaten

this book is mine
that book is his
this book is ours
I am your friend
here
now
that
there
then

The Girls

Margru, Teme, Kere,
the three little girls onboard.
In Connecticut
they stay with Pendleton
the jailer and his wife.
Some say they are slaves
in that house. The lawyer
comes to remove them,
but they cling to their hosts,
run screaming through the snow
instead of go. Cinque comes
and speaks in their language
with much agitation.
Do you fear Pendleton? *No.*
Do you fear the lawyer? *No.*
Do you fear Cinque? *No.*
Who or what do you fear?
The men, they say, *the men.*
The girls will become Christians.
They will move to Farmington
with the Mende mission
and return to Sierra Leone.
One will return to America
to attend college at Oberlin.
They will be called Sarah,
Maria, and Charlotte.

Kere's Song

My brother would gather the salt crust.
My grandmother would boil it gray to white.

My mother boated in the near salt river,
grabbed fat fish from the water with bare hands.

Women paint their faces with white clay and dance
to bring girls into our society, our

secrets, our womanhood, our community.
The clay-whitened faces of my mothers

are what I see in my dreams, and hear
drum-songs that drown girls' cries after

they have been cut to be made women.
If someone does evil, hags ride them

all night and pummel them to exhaustion.
Hags slip off their skins and leave them

in the corner during such rambles.
At my grandmother's grave, cooked chicken, red rice,

and water to sustain her on her journey.
I was learning the secrets of Sande

when they brought me here, before my dance,
before my drum, before my Sande song.

Judge Judson

These negroes are *bozals*
(those recently from Africa)
not *ladinos*

(those long on the island)
and were imported
in violation of the law.

The question remains:
What disposition shall be made
of these negroes?

Bloody may be their hands
yet they shall
embrace their kindred.

Cinqueze and Grabeau
shall not sigh for Africa
in vain

and once remanded
they shall no longer
be here.

In Cursive

Westville, February 9, 1841

Miss Chamberlain and others,

I will write you a few lines
because I love you very much
and I want you to pray to the great God to make us free
and give us new souls and pray for African people.

He sent his beloved son into the world
to save sinners who were lost. He sent
the Bible into the world to save us
from going down to Hell, to make us turn from sin.

I heard Mr Booth say you give five dollars
to Mr Townsend for African people. I thank you
and hope the great God will help you and bless you
and hear you and take you up to Heaven when you die.

I want you to pray to the great God make us free.
We want to go home and see our friends in African Country.
I want the great God love me very much and forgive all my sins.
All Mendi people thank you for your kindness.

Hope to meet you in Heaven. Your friend, Kale

God

There is one God in Farmington, Connecticut,
another in Mendeland.

None listen.
None laugh, but none have listened.

We will sail home carrying Bibles
and wearing calico.

The journey this time
is seven weeks.

If we find our mothers,
children, fathers, brothers,

sisters, aunties, uncles,
cousins, friends,

if we find them,
we will read to them

(we read this book)
the God stories in our Bibles.

That is the price for the ticket home
to Mendeland

for us the decimated three years hence.

Waiting for Cinque to Speak

Having tried,

having tried, having failed,

having raised rice
that shimmered green, green,
having planted and threshed.

Having been a man, having sired children,
having raised my rice, having amassed a bit of debt,
having done nothing remarkable.

Years later it would be said
the Africans were snatched into slavery, then,
that we were sold by our own into slavery, then,
that those of our own who sold us
never imagined chattel slavery,
the other side of the Atlantic.

Having amassed debt, I was taken to settle that debt.
(Not enough rice in the shimmering green.)
Better me than my daughter or son. (I was strong.)
And on the ship I met my day
as a man must meet his day.
Out of the Babel of Wolof and Kissee
we were made of the same flour and water, it happened.
On the ship, I met my day.

The *Amistad* Trail

The *Amistad* Trail bus
leaves from the commuter parking lot,
Exit 37 off Highway 84.
There is interest in this tale.

See where the girls lived while waiting
for the boat to sail home, see Cinque's room,
the Farmington church where they learned
to pray to Jesus, Foone's grave.

Good things: eventual justice, John Quincy Adams,
black fighting back, white helping black.
Bad things: the fact of it, price of the ticket,
the footnote, the twist, and the rest –

Done took my blues
Done took my blues and

– the good and the bad of it.
Preach it: learn. Teach it: weep.

Done took my blues.
Done took my blues and gone.
The verse will not resolve.
The blues that do not end.

Cinque Redux

I will be called bad motherfucker.
I will be venerated.
I will be misremembered.
I will be Seng-Pieh, Cinqueze, Joseph,
and end up CINQUE.

I will be remembered
as upstart, rebel, rabble-rouser, leader.
My name will be taken by black men
who wish to be thought RIGHTEOUS.
My portrait will be called 'The Black Prince'.
Violent acts will be committed in my name.
My face will appear on Sierra Leonean currency.

I will not proudly sail the ship home
but will go home, where I will not sell slaves,
then will choose to sail off
to a new place: Jamaica, West Indies.
In America, they called us *'Amistads'*.
The cook we killed, Celestino, was mulatto.
Many things are true at once.

Yes I drew my hand across my throat
in the courtroom, at that cur Ruiz
to hex his thieving, killing self.
Yes I scuffled here and there instead of immolate.
Yes I flaunted my gleam and spring.
No I did not smile.
No I never forgot the secret teachings
of my fathers. No I never forgot

who died on board, who died on land,
who did what to whom, who will die
in the future, which I see
unfurling like the strangest dream.

The Last Quatrain

and where now
and what now
the black white space

NOTE

On July 2, 1839, a rebellion occurred aboard the Spanish slave schooner *Amistad* near the coast of Cuba. The *Amistad* was sailing from Havana to Puerto Principe, Cuba, when the ship's passengers, three girls, one boy and thirty-nine men recently abducted from Sierra Leone, revolted. The captives, led by Joseph Cinque, killed the ship's captain and cook, but spared the navigator so that he would bring the ship back to Sierra Leone. Instead, the navigator sailed northward, where the United States Navy seized the *Amistad* off Long Island and towed it to New London, Connecticut. The captives were held in a jail in New Haven, Connecticut. There was great interest in their presence, including from Yale Professor Josiah Willard Gibbs, who brought his students to try to teach the captives English so that they might tell their story in court.

The Spanish demanded the return of the *Amistad* captives to Cuba. In 1840, a trial took place in a federal court in Hartford, Connecticut. New England abolitionist Lewis Tappan and others tried to organise sympathy for the captives, but the United States government sided with proslavery opinions. President Martin Van Buren ordered a Navy ship sent to Connecticut to return the Africans to Cuba. Nonetheless, the judge ruled that the captives were not merchandise, but were instead victims of kidnapping and had the right to escape their captors; he said they should be made free. The United States appealed the case before the Supreme Court the next year; congressmen and former president John Quincy Adams argued in favor of the Africans. The Supreme Court upheld the lower court. Private and missionary society donations helped the thirty-five surviving Africans secure passage back to Sierra Leone, where they arrived in January 1842. Five missionaries and teachers hoping to found a Christian mission joined the Africans on this return.

Spain insisted that the United States pay indemnification for the ship. The United States Congress continued to debate the case until the beginning of the Civil War in 1861.

American Sublime

(At the same time, American paintings wherein
the biodynamic landscape explodes in flames,

ice, violent sunshine that seems to burn the canvas,
apocalyptic nature that roils and terrifies.

The Beautiful: small scale, gentle luminosity.
Sublime: territorial, vast, craggy, un-

domesticated, borderless, immense, unknown,
awful, monumental, transcendent, transcending.

Go West and West young man, to blinding snowstorms. Leave
shark-infested waters, shipwrecks without slaves.

Miraculous black holes of color large enough
to blot out the sun, obliterate the unending moans,

to exalt, to take the place of lamentation.)

Tanner's Annunciation

Gabriel disembodied,
pure column of light.
Humble Mary, receiving the word
that the baby she carries is God's.
Not good news, not news, even,
but rather the rightly enormous word,
Annunciation. She knew
they were chosen. She knew
he would suffer, as the chosen child
always suffers. Perhaps she knew
the dearest wish, mercy,
would be ever-inchoate,
like Gabriel: light that carries
possibility, illuminates,
but that can promise nothing but itself.

from

ANTEBELLUM DREAMBOOK

(2001)

I had a dream, its voice spoke to me:
'Why don't you draw or die?'
'Is that it?', I said, 'My, My.'

MINNIE EVANS

Fugue

1 *Walking (1963)*

after the painting by Charles Alston

You tell me, knees are important, you kiss
your elders' knees in utmost reverence.

The knees in this painting are what send the people forward.

Once progress felt real and inevitable,
as sure as the taste of licorice or lemons.
The painting was made after marching
in Birmingham, walking

into a light both brilliant and unseen.

2 *1964*

In a beige silk sari
my mother danced the frug
to the Peter Duchin Band.

Earlier that day
at Maison Le Pelch
the French ladies twisted

her magnificent hair
into a fat chignon
while mademoiselle watched,

drank sugared, milky tea,
and counted bobby pins
disappearing in the thick-

ness as the ladies worked
in silence, adornment
so grave, the solemn toilette,

and later, the bath,
and later, red lipstick,
and later, L'Air de Temps.

My mother without glasses.
My mother in beige silk.
My mother with a chignon.
My mother in her youth.

3 *1968*

The city burns. We have to stay at home,
TV always interrupted with fire or helicopters.
Men who have tweedled my cheeks once or twice
join the serial dead.

Yesterday I went downtown with Mom.
What a pretty little girl, said the tourists, who were white.
My shoes were patent leather, all shiny, and black.
My father is away saving the world for Negroes,
I wanted to say.

Mostly I go to school or watch television
with my mother and brother, my father often gone.
He makes the world a better place for Negroes.
The year is nineteen-sixty-eight.

4 *1971*

'Hey Blood,' my father said then
to other brothers in the street.
'Hey, Youngblood, how you doin'?

'Peace and power,' he says,
and, 'Keep on keepin' on,'
just like Gladys Knight and the Pips.

My stomach jumps: a thrill.
Sometimes poems remember small things, like
'Hey, Blood.' My father
still says that sometimes.

5 *The Sun King (1974)*

James Hampton, the Sun King
of Washington, DC
erects a tinfoil throne.
'Where there is no vision, the people perish.'
Altar, pulpit, lightbulbs.

My 14th and 'U', my 34 bus, my weekday winos,
my white-robed black Israelites
on their redstone stoops,
my graffiti: 'Anna the Leo as "Ice" ',
my neon James Brown poster
coming to the DC Coliseum
where all I will see is the circus,
my one visit to RKO Keith's Theater
to see *Car Wash*
and a bird flew in, and mania,
frantic black shadow on the screen,
I was out of the house in a theater full of black folks,
black people, black movie, black bird,
I was out, I was free, I was at RKO Keith's Theater
at 14th and 'U'
and it was not *Car Wash* it was the first
Richard Pryor concert movie
and a bird flew in the screen
and memory is romance
and race is romance,
and the Sun King lives
in Washington, DC.

Early Cinema

According to Mister Hedges, the custodian
who called upon their parents
after young Otwiner and young Julia
were spotted at the matinee
of Rudolph Valentino in *The Sheik*
at the segregated Knickerbocker Theater
in the uncommon Washington December
of 1922, 'Your young ladies
were misrepresenting themselves today',
meaning, of course, that they were passing.
After coffee and no cake were finished
and Mister Hedges had buttoned his coat
against the strange evening chill,
choice words were had with Otwiner and Julia,
shame upon the family, shame upon the race.

How they'd longed to see Rudolph Valentino,
who was swarthy like a Negro, like the finest Negro man.
In *The Sheik*, they'd heard, he was turbaned,
whisked damsels away in a desert cloud.
They'd heard this from Lucille and Ella
who'd put on their fine frocks and French,
claiming to be 'of foreign extraction'
to sneak into the Knickerbocker Theater
past the usher who knew their parents
but did not know them.
They'd heard this from Mignon and Doris
who'd painted carmine bindis on their foreheads
braided their black hair tight down the back,
and huffed, 'We'll have to take this up with the Embassy'
to the squinting ticket taker.
Otwiner and Julia were tired of Oscar Michaux,
tired of church, tired of responsibility,
rectitude, posture, grooming, modulation,
tired of homilies each way they turned,
tired of colored right and wrong.
They wanted to be whisked away.

The morning after Mister Hedges' visit
the paperboy cried 'Extra!' and Papas
shrugged camel's hair topcoats over pressed pajamas,
and Mamas read aloud at the breakfast table,
'No Colored Killed When Roof Caves In'
at the Knickerbocker Theater
at the evening show
from a surfeit of snow on the roof.
One hundred others dead.

It appeared that God had spoken.
There was no school that day,
no movies for months after.

Visitor

Belo Horizonte

The city rocks at close of day,
buses lumber, workers hustle home.
Sunlight's a silt on these buildings
outside my hotel window. I am high up,
a visitor to this new city, excited
and weary as Lorca or Senghor. Here,
they say it straight: white women
to marry, black women for work,
mulattas for fucking. There are hundreds
of words describing color, skin, and who
I would be in this city is unclear.

A car horn plays 'La Cucaracha',
just like Uptown, USA. Streetlights
and headlights appear like chicken pox.
I could look out this window for hours
at the finishing day, the lancets
and whippets of shiny rose light.
My eyes are a gemologist's, divining
mica from mud, mining iridescence,
a country, composed in legible lumens, color.

Days later on the night-flight,
almost West and home, the wide sky wakes.
America becomes visible beneath plush clouds
outside bituminous Pittsburgh,
gray and mottled, gridless, dappled.

Then the clouds clot and we are in heaven.

I am black again. The sky is pale and pink.

My suitcase is full of poems in Portuguese,
beads to protect me that will break in a month,
vacuum-packed coffee beans, ebony fists,
black soap that lathers up creamy, and white.

Islands Number Four

1

Agnes Martin, *Islands Number Four*,
Repeated ovals on a grid, what appears
To be perfect is handmade, disturbed.
Tobacco brown saturates canvas to burlap,
Clean form from a distance, up close, her hand.
All wrack and bramble to oval and grid.
Hollows in the body, containers for grief.
What looks to be perfect is not perfect.

Odd oval portholes that flood with light.

2

Description of a Slave Ship, 1789:
Same imperfect ovals, calligraphic hand.
At a distance, pattern. Up close, bodies
Doubled and doubled, serried and stacked
In the manner of galleries in a church,
In full ships on their sides or on each other.
Isle of woe, two-by-two, spoon-fashion,
Not unfrequently found dead in the morning.
Slave ships, the not pure, imperfect ovals,
Portholes through which they would never see home,
The flesh rubbed off their shoulders, elbows, hips.
Barracoon, sarcophagus, indestructible grief
Nesting in the hollows of the abdomen.
The slave ship empty, its cargo landed
And sold for twelve ounces of gold apiece

Or gone overboard. Islands. Aftermath.

Nat Turner Dreams of Insurrection

...too much sense to be raised, and if I was,
I would never be of any service to any one as a slave.
THE CONFESSIONS OF NAT TURNER, 1831

Drops of blood on the corn, as dew from heaven.
Forms of men in different attitudes, portrayed in blood.
Numbers, glyphs, on woodland leaves, also in blood.

Freedom: a dipperful of cold well water.
Freedom: the wide white sky.
Dreams that make me sweat.

Because I am called, I must appear so, prepare.
I am not a conjurer. Certain marks on my head and breast.
Shelter me, Great Dismal Swamp. A green-blue sky which roils.

Race

Sometimes I think about Great-Uncle Paul who left Tuskegee,
Alabama to become a forester in Oregon and in so doing
became fundamentally white for the rest of his life, except
when he traveled without his white wife to visit his siblings –
now in New York, now in Harlem, USA – just as pale-skinned,
as straight-haired, as blue-eyed as Paul, and black. Paul never told anyone
he was white, he just didn't say that he was black, and who could imagine,
an Oregon forester in 1930 as anything other than white?
The siblings in Harlem each morning ensured
no one confused them for anything other than what they were, black.
They were black! Brown-skinned spouses reduced confusion.
Many others have told, and not told, this tale.
When Paul came East alone he was as they were, their brother.

The poet invents heroic moments where the pale black ancestor stands up
on behalf of the race. The poet imagines Great-Uncle Paul
in cool, sagey groves counting rings in redwood trunks,
imagines pencil markings in a ledger book, classifications,
imagines a sidelong look from an ivory spouse who is learning
her husband's caesuras. She can see silent spaces
but not what they signify, graphite markings in a forester's code.

Many others have told, and not told, this tale.
The one time Great-Uncle Paul brought his wife to New York
he asked his siblings not to bring their spouses,
and that is where the story ends: ivory siblings who would not
see their brother without their telltale spouses.
What a strange thing is "race", and family, stranger still.
Here a poem tells a story, a story about race.

Gravitas

Emergency! A bright yellow school bus
is speeding me to hospital. My pregnant belly bulges
beneath my pleated skirt, the face
of my dear niece Amal a locket inside my stomach.

Soon she will be born healthy,
and after, her sister, Bana.
Labor will be tidy and effortless.
In fact, I will hardly remember it!

All of this is taking place in Kenya, where they live.
This is my first dream of pregnancy
since I have been actually pregnant,
therefore I dream in reality rather than metaphor.

I am gravid, eight weeks along.
My baby, I have read, has a tail
and a spine made of pearls,
and every day I speak to her in tongues.

Crash

I am the last woman off of the plane
that has crashed in a cornfield near Philly,

picking through hot metal
for my rucksack and diaper bag.

No black box, no fuselage,
just sistergirl pilot wiping soot from her eyes,

happy to be alive. Her dreadlocks
will hold the smoke for weeks.

All the white passengers bailed out
before impact, so certain a sister

couldn't navigate the crash. O gender.
O race. O ye of little faith.

Here we are in the cornfield, bruised and dirty but alive.
I invite sistergirl pilot home for dinner

at my parents', for my mother's roast chicken
with gravy and rice, to celebrate.

Nat King Cole on the Amalfi Drive

He sings after making the beast with two backs,
something low-down and dirty, fried liver and onions,
put your hands on your hips and let your diction slip.

We do it real quick. I am 'that kind of girl'.
He shakes out his marcel, calls Yes!
to the Lord, caretaker of bliss, maker of figs,

the good Lord of smothered chicken and biscuits
who gave us five senses, said, Go forth and taste
for your time on this earth is not long.

We keep our pleasure secret, dahlias
underneath my skirt as I watch from the studio audience.
The Negro crooner sings of 'Eskeemos'.

Wild applause from the flush-cheeked fans.
My dahlias rustle, brush. A wink for me,
a smile for me, for me in black and white.

The Toni Morrison Dreams

1

Toni Morrison despises
conference coffee, so I offer
to fetch her a Starbucks
macchiato grande, with turbinado sugar.

She's delighted, can start her day properly,
draws on her Gauloises,
shakes her gorgeous, pewter dreads,
sips the java that I brought her
and reads her own words:

Nuns go by as quiet as lust

Everything in silver-gray and black.

2 *Workshop*

She asks us to adapt
Synge's *Playboy of the Western World*
for the contemporary stage.
She asks us to translate *The Birds*.

She asks us to think about clocks,
see the numbers as glyphs,
consider the time we spend watching them

in class, on line, at the hairdresser's.

In class she calls me 'Ouidah' and I answer.

'I am the yellow mother
of two yellow boys,' she says.
I sit up straight.

Now the work begins, and
Oh
the work is hard.

3

She does not love
my work, but she loves
my baby, tells me
to have many more.

4 *A Reading at Temple University*

'Love,' she wrote,
and 'love' and 'love' and 'love',

and 'amanuensis', 'velvet', 'pantry', 'lean',

Shadrack, Solomon, Hagar, Jadine, Plum,

circles   sth   runagate

and then,
she whispered it,

love

'The female seer will burn upon this pyre'

Sylvia Plath is setting my hair
on rollers made from orange-juice cans.
The hairdo is shaped like a pyre.

My locks are improbably long.
A pyramid of lemons somehow
balances on the rickety table

where we sit, in the rented kitchen
which smells of singed naps and bergamot.
Sylvia Plath is surprisingly adept

at rolling my unruly hair.
She knows to pull it tight.
                                        Few words.

Her flat, American belly,

her breasts in a twin sweater set,
stack of typed poems on her desk,
envelopes stamped to go by the door,

a freshly baked poppyseed cake,
kitchen safety matches, black-eyed Susans
in a cobalt jelly jar. She speaks a word,

'immolate', then a single sentence
of prophecy. The hairdo done,
the nursery tidy, the floor swept clean

of burnt hair and bumblebee husks.

War

In the dream there was goo,
yellow goo which hurled itself
at unclothed bodies, and burned.
Shower water slowing to a trickle,
mayhem on TV and on the radio.

Dan Rather in slow motion:
We thought they'd attack
a medium-sized city of poor people,
like Philadelphia,
not a mighty city like Chicago.

Tanks, firing with no sound.
Mayhem, a word I've been drawn to
for the last week for no apparent reason,
my newest, pulsing word
in a dream where I do not picture enemies.

Peccant

Maryland State Correctional Facility for Women,
Baltimore County Branch, has undergone a face-lift.
Cells are white and ungraffitied, roomlike, surprisingly airy.
This is where I must spend the next year, eating slop from tin trays,
facing women much tougher than I am, finding out if I am brave.
Though I do not know what I took, I know I took something.

On Exercise Day, walk the streets of the city you grew up in,
in my case, DC, from pillar to post, Adams-Morgan to Anacostia,
Shaw to Southwest, Logan to Chevy Chase Circles,
recalling every misbegotten everything, lamenting, repenting.

How my parents keen and weep, scheme to spring me,
intercept me at corners with bus tokens, pass keys, files baked in cakes.
Komunyakaa the poet says, don't write what you know,
write what you are willing to discover, so I will
spend this year, these long days, meditating on what I am accused of
in the white rooms, city streets, communal showers, mess hall,
where all around me sin and not sin is scraped off tin trays
into oversized sinks, all that excess, scraped off and rinsed away.

After the Gig: Mick Jagger

The baby cries. Mick Jagger swaggers backstage,
lit with sweat. The crowd still screams outside.
He's been second-lining with a gaggle of New Orleans Negroes,
a white parasol, wears toreador pants and is
bare-chested, bones.

I've forgiven the Rolling Stones for fetishising me
and my sisters in 'Brown Sugar' and 'Some Girls'.
Black girls, black girls, black girls.
Why does so much flotsam populate my brain?
Why not ancient Ge'ez, the Mingus discography,

suminagashi paper technique,

something utilitarian?

This is a four weeks postpartum dream. Mick Jagger's
black baby cries again. Thank God, it isn't mine.
Gotta go, love, gotta go, he says,
and shrugs his bony shoulders,
grins that reptile-mammal grin,

picks the baby up, coo-coos,

and then rocks that baby down.

Visitation

Pablo Neruda still lives in my dream,
will discuss with me a better language
for poems both 'political' and 'personal',
dandles my poppy-faced baby on his knee,
offers to blurb my latest collection,
prefers English to Spanish this bright afternoon
(but oh how my Spanish glitters in this dream!).
I remember to him his great poems, muses:
Matilde Urrutia, 'Amores: Josie Bliss', 'Walking Around',
lines that made the words inside me shift and organise.
He understands why I fall asleep sometimes
when Important Visitors lecture at the University.
Of course you fall asleep, he says, and waves.
Adios, cariña. You're off to write a poem.

Feminist Poem Number One

Yes I have dreams where I am rescued by men:
my father, brother, husband, no one else.
Last night I dreamed my brother and husband
morphed into each other and rescued me
from a rat-infested apartment. 'Run!'
he said, feral scampering at our heels.
And then we went to lunch at the Four Seasons.

What does it mean to be a princess?
'I am what is known as an American Negro,'
my grandmother would say, when 'international friends'
would ask her what she was. She'd roller-skate
to Embassy Row and sit on the steps of the embassies
to be certain the rest of the world was there.

What does it mean to be a princess?
My husband drives me at 6 A.M.
to the airport an hour away, drives home,
drives back when I have forgotten my passport.
What does it mean to be a prince? I cook
savory, fragrant meals for my husband
and serve him, if he likes, in front of the TV.
He cooks for me, too. I have a husband.

In the dream we run into Aunt Lucy,
who is waiting for a plane from 'Abyssinia'
to bring her lover home. I am the one
married to an Abyssinian, who is already here. I am the one
with the grandmother who wanted to know the world.
I am what is known as an American Negro princess,
married to an African prince,
living in a rat-free apartment in New Haven,
all of it, all of it, under one roof.

Narrative: Ali

a poem in twelve rounds

1

My head so big
they had to pry
me out. I'm sorry
Bird (is what I call
my mother). Cassius
Marcellus Clay,
Muhammad Ali;
you can say
my name in any
language, any
continent: Ali.

2

Two photographs
of Emmett Till,
born my year,
on my birthday.
One, he's smiling,
happy, and the other one
is after. His mother
did the bold thing,
kept the casket open,
made the thousands look upon
his bulging eyes,
his twisted neck,
her lynched black boy.
I couldn't sleep
for thinking,
Emmett Till.

One day I went
down to the train tracks,
found some iron

shoe-shine rests
and planted them
between the ties
and waited
for a train to come,
and watched the train
derail, and ran,
and after that
I slept at night.

3

I need to train
around people,
hear them talk,
talk back. I need
to hear the traffic,
see people in
the barbershop,
people getting
shoe shines, talking,
hear them talk,
talk back.

4

Bottom line: Olympic gold
can't buy a black man
a Louisville hamburger
in nineteen-sixty.

Wasn't even real gold.
I watched the river
drag the ribbon down,
red, white, and blue.

5

Laying on the bed,
praying for a wife,
in walk Sonji Roi.

Pretty little shape.
Do you like
chop suey?

Can I wash your hair
underneath
that wig?

Lay on the bed,
Girl. Lie
with me.

Shake to the east,
to the north,
south, west –

but remember,
remember, I need
a Muslim wife. So

Quit using lipstick.
Quit your boogaloo.
Cover up your knees

like a Muslim
wife, religion,
religion, a Muslim

wife. Eleven
months with Sonji,
first woman I loved.

6

There's not
too many days
that pass that I
don't think
of how it started,
but I know
no Great White Hope
can beat
a true black champ.
Jerry Quarry
could have been
a movie star,
a millionaire,
a senator,
a president –
he only had
to do one thing,
is whip me,
but he can't.

7 *Dressing-room Visitor*

He opened
up his shirt:
'KKK' cut
in his chest.
He dropped
his trousers:
latticed scars
where testicles
should be. His face
bewildered, frozen,
in the Alabama woods
that night in 1966
when they left him
for dead, his testicles
in a Dixie cup.

You a warning,
they told him,
to smart-mouth,
sassy-acting niggers,
meaning niggers
still alive,
meaning any nigger,
meaning niggers
like me.

8 *Training*

Unsweetened grapefruit juice
will melt my stomach down.
Don't drive if you can walk,
don't walk if you can run.
I add a mile each day
and run in eight-pound boots.

My knuckles sometimes burst
the glove. I let dead skin
build up, and then I peel it,
let it scar, so I don't bleed
as much. My bones
absorb the shock.

I train in three-minute
spurts, like rounds: three
rounds big bag, three speed
bag, three jump rope, one-
minute breaks,
no more, no less.

Am I too old? Eat only
kosher meat. Eat cabbage,
carrots, beets, and watch
the weight come down:
two-thirty, two-twenty,
two-ten, two-oh-nine.

9

Will I go
like Kid Paret,
a fractured
skull, a ten-day
sleep, dreaming
alligators, pork
chops, saxophones,
slow grinds, funk,
fishbowls, lightbulbs,
bats, typewriters,
tuning forks, funk,
clocks, red rubber
ball, what you see
in that lifetime
knockout minute
on the cusp?
You could be
let go,
you could be
snatched back.

10 *Rumble in the Jungle*

Ali boma ye,
Ali boma ye,
means kill him, Ali,
which is different
from a whupping
which is what I give,
but I lead them chanting
anyway, Ali
boma ye, because
here in Africa
black people fly
planes and run countries.

I'm still making up
for the foolishness
I said when I was
Clay from Louisville,
where I learned Africans
lived naked in straw
huts eating tiger meat,
grunting and grinning,
swinging from vines,
pounding their chests –

I pound my chest but of my own accord.

11

I said to Joe Frazier,
first thing, get a good house
in case you get crippled
so you and your family
can sleep somewhere. Always
keep one good Cadillac.
And watch how you dress
with that cowboy hat,
pink suits, white shoes –
that's how pimps dress,
or kids, and you a champ,
or wish you were, 'cause
I can whip you in the ring
or whip you in the street.
Now back to clothes,
wear dark clothes, suits,
black suits, like you the best
at what you do, like you
President of the World.
Dress like that.
Put them yellow pants away.
We dinosaurs gotta
look good, gotta sound
good, gotta be good,
the greatest, that's what

I told Joe Frazier,
and he said to me,
we both bad niggers.
We don't do no crawlin'.

12

They called me 'the fistic pariah'.

They said I didn't love my country,
called me a race-hater, called me out
of my name, waited for me
to come out on a stretcher, shot at me,
hexed me, cursed me, wished me
all manner of ill will,
told me I was finished.

Here I am,
like the song says,
come and take me,

'The People's Champ',

myself,
Muhammad.

Neonatology

Is
funky, is
leaky, is
a soggy, bloody crotch, is
sharp jets of breast milk shot straight across the room,
is gaudy, mustard-colored poop, is
postpartum tears that soak the baby's lovely head.
Then everything dries and disappears
Then everything dries and disappears
Neonatology
is day into night into day,
light into dark into light, semi-
and full-fledged, hyperconscious,
is funky, is funny: the baby farts,
we laugh. The baby burps, we smile, say 'Yes'.
The baby poops, his whole body stiffens,
then steam heat floods the pipes.
He slashes his nose with nails we cannot bear to trim,
takes a nap, and the wounds disappear.
The spirit lives in your squirts and coos.
Your noises and fluids are what you do.
Neonatology
is what we cannot see: you speak to the birds,
the birds speak back, is solemn,
singing, funky, frightening,
buckets of tears on the baby's lovely head, is

spongy.

*

'One day you'll forget the baby,' Mother says,
'as if he were a pocketbook, a bag of groceries,
something you leave on a kitchen countertop.
I left you once, put on my coat and hat,
remembered my pocketbook, the top and bottom locks,
got all the way to the elevator before I realised.

It only happens once.'

*

We lay on the bed and we rode the gray waves,
apricot juice in a glass in your hand,
single color in this gray light like November.
It is April. We rock.

Then the miracle which is always a miracle happens in many stages,

then the mouth which opens,
the bluebell
that sings.

I was just pregnant,
am no longer pregnant,
see myself in my memory
in overalls, sensible shoes.

*

Shockingly vital, mammoth giblet,
the second living thing to break free
of my body in fifteen minutes.

The midwife presents it on a platter.
We do not eat, have no Tupperware
to take it home and sanctify a tree.

Instead, we marvel at my cast-off meat,
the almost-pulsing slab, bloody mesa,
what lived moments ago and now has died.

Now I must take the baby to my breast.
There is no mother here but me.
The midwife discards the placenta.

*

What do you make of this rain, little one,
night rain that your parents have loved all their lives?

From 2 to 3 *The Streets of San Francisco* comes on each night,
and I watch Karl Malden stop crime, and listen

to the mouse-squeak of your suckling, behold your avid jaws,
your black eyes: otter, ocelot,

my whelp, my cub, my seapup.
In the days before you smile at me

or call me Mama or love me,
love is all tit, all wheat-smelling milk, humid crook of the arm

where your warm, damp head seems to live.
I pretend your clasping my finger means you love me.

*

Dreamt the baby
was born again,
arrived this time in a Moses basket,
had a crone's face,
a Senegalese head wrap,
a pendulous lower lip.

*

Mamma Zememesh, I dreamt your sister's names.
They floated around me as objects, satellites:

Zayd
        Ntutu
                Yeshareg
                        Asefash
                                Moulounesh

a spinning, turning, turning, spin.

*

I think the baby needs to eat. The baby's hungry.
Look! He's making sucking noises. Look!
His fist is in his mouth.

Why does the baby sleep all day? How
does the baby sleep at night? Three feedings? Hunh.
You need to let that baby cry.
You need to pick that baby up.
You need to put that baby down.
Kiss the baby too much, he'll get heartburn.
What are those bumps on the baby's face?
Why is the baby crying so?
That baby needs to eat, and now.

*

I dream the OB-GYN is here
to spend the night with us. He wears
his white coat and his stethescope
to bed, looks like a loaf
of whole wheat bread. Goodnight, we say,
and shut our eyes.
                                        The next day
he's up early, jolly. 'Time
to have this baby! Tallyho!' And so we do.

*

All of my aunties chatting like crows on a line,
all of my aunties on electric breast pumps,
the double kind, one for each exhausted tit.

Mommy, the baby's head popped off! A tiny head,
white, wet, bloodless, heartbeat still on the soft spot.
She tells me, Stick it back on, Girl. Don't be afraid.

You can't show your children you're afraid.

A paraffin seam bubbles on his scalp.
A pink cicatrix lines his lovely neck.

*

Giving birth is like jazz, something from silence,
then all of it. Long, elegant boats,
blood-boiling sunshine, human cargo,
a handmade kite –

Postpartum.
No longer a celebrity, pregnant lady, expectant.
It has happened; you are here,
each dram you drain a step away
from flushed and floating, lush and curled.
Now you are the pink one, the movie star.
It has happened. You are here,

and you sing, mewl, holler, peep,
swallow the light and bubble it back,
shine, contain multitudes, gleam. You

are the new one, the movie star,
and birth is like jazz,
from silence and blood, silence
then everything,

jazz.

from

BODY OF LIFE

(1996)

Stravinsky in L.A.

In white pleated trousers, peering through green
sunshades, looking for the way the sun is red
noise, how locusts hiss to replicate the sun.
What is the visual equivalent
of syncopation? Rows of seared palms wrinkle
in the heat waves through green glass. Sprinklers
tick, tick, tick. The Watts Towers aim to split
the sky into chroma, spires tiled with rubble
nothing less than aspiration. I've left
minarets for sun and syncopation,
sixty-seven shades of green which I have
counted, beginning: palm leaves, front and back,
luncheon pickle, bottle glass, etcetera.
One day I will comprehend the different
grades of red. On that day I will comprehend
these people, rhythms, jazz, Simon Rodia,
Watts, Los Angeles, aspiration.

The Josephine Baker Museum

1 *East St Louis* (1918)

Mama danced
a glass
of water balanced
on her head.

'Someone raped
a white woman!'
We ran
at night,
next day
heard tell

of eyes
plucked out,
of scalps
pulled clean,
a bloody sky.

That day
God showed
his face,
grey and shaggy,
in the rain clouds.

2 *Costumes*

The black and white checked overalls
I wore off the boat at Le Havre. Wired skirts
whose trains weigh fifty pounds. Furling,
curling headpieces, and hourglass-
shaped gowns.

Schiaparellis and Poirets! The green suede
Pilgrim shoes and orange jacket,
Harlem-made. The lime chiffon!
the one with egrets
painted on.

I'm sick of *touts le bananes*. Ici,
my uniform: French Air Force, fray-spots
blackened back with ink. And here,
the diamond necklace,
for my glorious Chiquita.

3 *The Wig Room*

A gleaming black sputnik of hair.
A solid figure-eight of hair, glazed black.
Crows' wings of hair, a waist-length switch.

Black profiteroles of mounded hair.
Hair like an Eiffel Tower, painted black.
A ziggurat of patent leather hair.

Black crowns to be taken on and off, that live
in the room when the lights go out, a roomful
of whispering Josephines, a roomful
of wigs in the dark.

4 *Ablutions*

In the cinema Mammy hands Scarlett
white underthings to cover her white skin.
I am both of them and neither, tall,
tan, terrific, soaking in my tub of milk.

What would it mean to be me on stage
in a bathtub soaping, singing my French
chansons with one pointed foot with painted toes
suggesting what is underneath, suggesting

dusky, houri dreams and is she really
naked? Do they really want to see
the nappy pussy underneath that sweats
and stinks and grinds beneath bananas,

turns to seaweed in the tub? What if
I let my hair go back, or dressed

more often as a man? What if I let myself
get fat? What would it mean to step out

of the bathtub onto the stage and touch
myself, do to myself what I do to myself
in the bedroom when only my animals
watch? What would I be to my audience then?

(Sigh) Come here, baby. Dry me off.

5 *Diva Studies*

What is original, what
is facsimile? The boys
in the dressing-room are showing
me how to skin my hair down flat
like patent leather, black as that.
I show them how to paint eyeballs
on their eyelids to look bright
from the last row, how I line
my eyes like the Egyptian cat.
We carry on, in that dingy,
musky, dusty room overhung
with fraying costumes, peeling
sequins, shedding feathers, mules
with broken heels, mending glue, eye-
lash glue, charcoal sticks and matches,
brushes and unguents and bottles of oil.
The dressing-room is my schoolhouse.
My teachers are men more woman
than actual women, and I
am the skinny sixteen-year-old
whose hair is slicked flat because
Congoleum burned it off.
I cross my eyes and knock my knees,
am somehow still a diva.
The boys swoop past and are rare.
The beauty is how this strange
trade works. The truth of it is,
we are fabulous.

Fugue

Virginia Woolf, incested
through her childhood, wrote
that she imagined herself
growing up inside a grape.
Grapes are sealed and safe.
You wouldn't quite float
in one; you'd sit locked
in enough moisture to keep
from drying out, the world
outside through gelid green.
Picture everyone's edges
smudged. Picture everyone
a green as delicate
as a Ming celadon. Pic-
ture yourself a mollusk
with an unsegmented body
in a skin so tight and taut
that you'd be safe. You could
ruminate all night about
the difference between 'taut'
and 'tight', 'molest' and 'incest'.
'Taut' means tightly-drawn,
high-strung. What is tight
is structured so as not to
permit passage of liquid
or gas, air, or light.

Passage

Henry Porter wore good clothes for his journey,
the best his wife could make from leftover
cambric, shoes stolen from the master. They
bit his feet, but if he took them off he feared
he'd never get them on again. He needed
to look like a free man when he got there.
Still in a box in the jostling heat,
nostrils to a board pried into a vent,
(a peephole, too, he'd hoped, but there was only
black to see) there was nothing to do
but sleep and dream and weep. Sometimes the dreams
were frantic, frantic loneliness an acid
at his heart. Freedom was near but un-
imaginable. Anxiety roiled inside
of him, a brew which corroded his stomach,
whose fumes clamped his lungs and his throat.
When the salt-pork and cornbread were finished
he dreamed of cream and eggs but the dreams
made him sick. He soiled himself and each time
was ashamed. He invented games, tried to
remember everything his mother
ever told him, every word he hadn't
understood, every vegetable he'd ever
eaten (which was easy: kale, okra, corn,
carrots, beans, chard, yams, dandelion greens),
remember everyone's name who had ever
been taken away. The journey went that way.
When he got there, his suit was chalky
with his salt, and soiled, the shoes waxy with blood.
The air smelled of a surfeit of mackerel.
Too tired to weep, too tired to look through
the peephole and see what freedom looked like,
he waited for the man to whom he'd shipped
himself: Mister William Still, Undertaker,
Philadelphia. He repeated the last
words he'd spoken to anyone: goodbye
wife Clothilde, daughter Eliza,
best friend Luke. Goodbye, everyone, goodbye.
When I can, I'll come for you. I swear,
I'll come for you.

Bossa Nova

The color green
which is the backdrop
for the whipped cream-

covered woman
on the jacket
of Brasil '66,

Herb Alpert and
the Tijuana Brass.
The woman puts one

whipped-cream finger
to her tongue,
which is red and I

imagine prickly. It
is nineteen-sixty-six
and this is Sexy.

Remember those hips-
ter horns, Brasil
for beginners, Oh!

I was born during
the bossa nova craze.
In nineteen sixty-six

I was four years old
and this was the record
that made me dance.

Apollo

We pull off
to a road shack
in Massachusetts
to watch men walk

on the moon. We did
the same thing
for three two one
blast off, and now

we watch the same men
bounce in and out
of craters. I want
a Coke and a hamburger.

Because the men
are walking on the moon
which is now irrefutably
not green, not cheese,

not a shiny dime floating
in a cold blue,
the way I'd thought,
the road shack people don't

notice we are a black
family not from there,
the way it mostly goes.
This talking through

static, bouncing in space-
boots, tethered
to cords is much
stranger, stranger

even than we are.

What I'm Telling You

If I say, my father was Betty Shabazz's lawyer, the poem can go no further. I've given you the punchline. If you know who she is, all you can think about is how and what you want to know about me, about my father, about Malcolm especially in 1990 when he's all over t-shirts and medallions, but what I'm telling you is that Mrs Shabazz was a nice lady to me, and I loved her name for the wrong reasons, SHABAZZ! and what I remember is going to visit her daughters in 1970 in a dark house with little furniture and leaving with a candy necklace the daughters gave me, to keep. Now that children see his name and call him, Malcolm Ten, and someone called her Mrs Ex-es, and they don't really remember who he was or what he said or how he smiled the way it happened when it did, and neither do I, I think about how history is made more than what happened and about a nice woman in a dark house filled with daughters and candy, something dim and unspoken, expectation.

Butter

My mother loves butter more than I do,
more than anyone. She pulls chunks off
the stick and eats it plain, explaining
cream spun around into butter! Growing up
we ate turkey cutlets sautéed in lemon
and butter, butter and cheese on green noodles,
butter melting in small pools in the hearts
of Yorkshire puddings, butter better
than gravy staining white rice yellow,
butter glazing corn in slipping squares,
butter the lava in white volcanoes
of hominy grits, butter softening
in a white bowl to be creamed with white
sugar, butter disappearing into
whipped sweet potatoes, with pineapple,
butter melted and curdy to pour
over pancakes, butter licked off the plate
with warm Alaga syrup. When I picture
the good old days I am grinning greasy
with my brother, having watched the tiger
chase his tail and turn to butter. We are
Mumbo and Jumbo's children despite
historical revision, despite
our parent's efforts, glowing from the inside
out, one hundred megawatts of butter.

My Grandmother's New York Apartment

1 *Apartment*

Everything pulled out or folded away:
sofa into a bed, tray tables that dis-
appear behind a door, everything
transmutable, alchemy in small
spaces, even my grandmother tiny
and changeable: a housecoat and rollers
which vanish and become an Irish
tweed suit, a tilted chapeau, a Hello
in the elevator just like, as she
would say, the Queen of Denmark.

2 *Bathroom*

Cuticle cream and orange sticks, bath oil pearls,
cotton wisps, boxed perfume in a lower
drawer, wire rollers, seaweedy stockings
drying on a rod, white garter belts,

white cotton gloves and Vaseline at night,
nail lacquer, tweezers, red lipsticks.
Push against your front teeth so they don't
go buck. Grease elbows, hair-ends, kneecaps, lips.

Grandmother smoked on the toilet at night.
Stop chewing your nails, stop picking your face.
Here is a diamond-dust fingernail file.
Your brand new rain-bonnet lost already?

Blues

I am lazy, the laziest
girl in the world. I sleep during
the day when I want to, till
my face is creased and swollen,
till my lips are dry and hot. I
eat as I please: cookies and milk
after lunch, butter and sour cream
on my baked potato, foods that
slothful people eat, that turn
yellow and opaque beneath the skin.
Sometimes come dinnertime Sunday
I am still in my nightgown, the one
with the lace trim listing because
I have not mended it. Many days
I do not exercise, only
consider it, then rub my curdy
belly and lie down. Even
my poems are lazy. I use
syllabics instead of iambs,
prefer slant- to the gong of full rhyme,
write briefly while others go
for pages. And yesterday,
for example, I did not work at all!
I got in my car and I drove
to factory outlet stores, purchased
stockings and panties and socks
with my father's money.

To think, in childhood I missed only
one day of school per year. I went
to ballet class four days a week
at four-forty-five and on
Saturdays, beginning always
with plie, ending with curtsy.
To think, I knew only industry,
the industry of my race
and of immigrants, the radio
tuned always to the station
that said, Line up your summer

job months in advance. Work hard
and do not shame your family,
who worked hard to give you what you have.
There is no sin but sloth. Burn
to a wick and keep moving.

I avoided sleep for years,
up at night replaying
evening news stories about
nearby jailbreaks, fat people
who ate fried chicken and woke up
dead. In sleep I am looking
for poems in the shape of open
V's of birds flying in formation,
or open arms saying, I forgive you, all.

Affirmative Action Blues (1993)

Right now two black people sit in a jury room
in Southern California trying to persuade
nine white people that what they saw when four white
police officers brought batons back like
they were smashing a beautiful piñata was
'a violation of Rodney King's civil rights',
just as I am trying to convince my boss not ever
to use the word 'niggardly' in my presence again.
He's a bit embarrassed, then asks, but don't you know
the word's etymology? as if that makes it
somehow not the word, as if a word can't batter.
Never again for as long as you live, I tell him,
and righteously. Then I dream of a meeting
with my colleagues where I scream so loud the inside
of my skull bleeds, and my face erupts in scabs.
In the dream I use an office which is overrun
with mice, rats, and round-headed baby otters
who peer at me from exposed water pipes (and somehow
I know these otters are Negroes), and my boss says,
Be grateful, your office is bigger than anyone
else's, and maybe if you kept it clean you wouldn't
have those rats. And meanwhile, black people are dying,
beautiful black men my age, from AIDS. It was amazing
when I learned the root of 'venereal disease'
was 'Venus', that there was such a thing as a disease
of love. And meanwhile, poor Rodney King can't think straight;
what was knocked into his head was some addled notion
of love his own people make fun of, 'Can we all
get along? Please?' You can't hit a lick with a crooked
stick; a straight stick made Rodney King believe he was
not a piñata, that amor vincit omnia.
I know I have been changed by love.
I know that love is not a political agenda, it lacks sustained
analysis, and we can't dance our way out of our constrictions.
I know that the word 'niggardly' is 'of obscure etymology' but
probably derived from the French Norman, and that
Chaucer and Milton and Shakespeare used it. It means
'stingy', and the root is not the same as 'nigger', which
derives from 'negar', meaning black, but they are perhaps,

perhaps, etymologically related. The two ‘g’s are two teeth gnawing; rodent is from the Latin ‘rodere’ which means ‘to gnaw’, as I have said elsewhere.
I know so many things, including the people who love me and the people who do not.
In Tourette’s syndrome you say the very thing that you are thinking, and then a word is real.
These are words I have heard in the last 24 hours which fascinate me: ‘vermin’, ‘screed’, ‘carmine’, and ‘niggardly’.
I am not a piñata, Rodney King insists. Now can’t we all get along?

For Miriam

Fields of iridescent, butter-lettuce green:
Germany a bright tail behind me
as I ride the train into Amsterdam's

impossible dipthongs, yellow or blue
'g's stopping words in new places. Poets
travel and make poems about travel,

grasp at their travels as I do here.
'Land' was a word for 'elsewhere' I used
in childhood, for storybook places where

other people lived. Italy: gondoliers
in tight, striped shirts, land of red and green noodles.
England: land of kings and queens, Elizabeth's

ermine-trimmed cape, her scepter and tiara,
Henry tearing at an outsized drumstick,
Germany: Adolf Hitler, mustachioed

Lucifer from another land, the Black
Forest where the Nazis had their revels,
my grandmother said. Now I have seen

Berlin's bullet-pocked buildings, the proud, scarred
church downtown, bolts of starry yellow fabric
stamped 'JUDE' in black, train schedules and ledgers

a rage of numbers, a cemetery
of Saras. In a bombed-out lot at dusk, art
made of rubble rose from smoke and rap music.

I've drunk green, herb-tinted beer, eaten bags
of local cherries and light-brown bread;
been jostled in a market jazzed with

turmeric, pistachios, raw fish,
hemp and honey soaps, silver trinkets;
sweated in a hammam where Turkish women

dance naked for each other in the steam.
I know, this is hardly the sum of it.
In my Berlin dreams, Jesse Owens' legs

are a brown flurry speeding past the Führer
in the name of another tribe, my own.
Here we talked about history, history,

history, which country forgets more, denies
more, and what is to be salvaged, in whose name?
Star-white jasmine, train-tracks without end –

This is what I have seen in your country, friend.

Body of Life

1 *1990*

One by one till
I'm the only one
left in the photo
we took in Gay Paree,
trill the final syl-
lable, thrill to
pretending we're
the Revue Negre,
funking so fiercely
our black clothes stained
our curvature, fab-
ulous flames let loose
in the city of lights.

One by one you leave
the picture, nix nix nix,
my moonpie face left
shining there. Au Revoir,
or like they say
in Sula, 'Vwah!', bright
as a bottle, the beau-
tiful children are
leaving me to trill
the final syllable,
this beautiful-
ugly world.

2 *1983*

The other girls taught shy me to be a diva,
to preen, to plump my titties up like they did,
to work it. We danced. We wanted the body
of life and I lived for a year in that
body, the body of life, in DC,
in the African diaspora:
Chocolate City.

That was my slut year.
All the men I didn't sleep with, all I did,
all the lunch dates, all the dinners, all
the whistles on the streets of Chocolate
City, all the men who called me Baby,
called me Girl, like the one who made me tuna-
fish and tried to suck my breasts, then asked
me to type up his résumé. My buzzer
in the middle of the night, my phone, a man
who greased me head to toe with Lubriderm,
a Cape Verdean who appeared on buses
and trains as if by divination, sketched
me naked, never spent the night. I told
one man how much I loved Betty Carter
and he said, I hope you're not one of those
bulldaggers. A lonely Nigerian
who cooked fufu and groped me on the sofa,
his across-the-ocean wife and daughter
watching from their picture frames.
Rum and dancing, too many things in my mouth,
genitals cobbled with passion or disease, bright
clitoris a phantom limb, remembering –

I moved away to Boston and would call
you for the update: Renee was a samba
star at Brasil Tropical, shimmied
on Brazilian TV. Denise graduated
school and made the foreign service, moved
to Jamaica, to a bungalow, with
a man and a maid named Pansy. 'Who's sick?'
I'd ask and you'd tell me, and who died,
and one day you said, 'And I'm living with AIDS.'

There was Kemron in Kenya.
You were saving to get it.
You met with a support group
of other black men. You had
a Dominican boyfriend,
same as me. Mostly you felt
OK, but you hated
your medicine. You were fat,
but you still took class.
No, Tyrone wasn't sick. But David was dead.

It was Njambi who called me to say,
you were back in shape. You performed
for the visiting Eminence of Senegal,
the next day went into the hospital,
the next day died. It made a romantic
story, but you're still gone. 'I love when you call me
because you're alive,' you said once,
one of your few friends still alive.
I'm writing this poem to say how we were,
that we danced and fucked and sweated, loved
ourselves and each other, lived fiercely,
knew joy. I'm writing to say,
I got lucky, you were my friend, you
knew me as a girl, I am a woman,
now, with my little piece of your story,
the year of the body of life.

3 *1994*

(In my neighborhood now I watch women who are lovely at a distance and lurid up close cross the street serving much runway, much attitude, and I am Ovaltine, a walrus, no longer sharp and spangled. In my half-sleep I hear teeth sucking from the dead, the divas awakening to coach me: Never let on you are less than fabulous, one says, hissing in disgust at all the home-training I've forgotten, so I pull myself together and whistle, a bald, brown, and beautiful Yul Brynner singing Deborah Kerr's lines: Whenever I feel afraid, I hold my head erect, and whistle a happy tune, so no one will suspect I'm afraid.

Life is only momentarily fearless; life is only for a moment full of cures; the body, as always, tells the round, bald truth when my stomach grips to say, no cure in sight.)

Dream

You come back from the evil where you've been so long
living and dying in a crusty, tired voice,
come back to hold me and tell me goodbye
in the Daskalides voice I first knew, and loved.
You take me to your bed and are suddenly naked,
and plump. You leave your glasses on. Your curls come back.
Then your best friend comes into the bed, who is my friend,
too, who is not yet sick but will be, and we lie
together, all of us naked and beautiful.
I smell your shit faintly, like a lover's known smells
toward the end of the day, like we know and love
and smell New York City – your penis bleeds a little
and your best friend licks it healed.

This is where it all
began: with love and ecstasy. I cry watching
these two men, the first tears because of it
since three years ago in a hotel lobby when
you told me everyone, everyone we knew
who was going to die of this. It was like
the awful first truth of childhood: yes, Mama will
die one day, but not for a long time, yes Daddy,
and dying is real, yes, you. That was when I used to dream
my family on the chain gang, in the desert, gone.
That was when I used to dream myself in a party dress
buckled to a chair inside a huge machine
which churned out shit. This is a new dream. I am grown.

We three are talking about poems, about Robert
Hayden's Coke-bottle glasses, about how the only time
he wrote of love it was lonely and austere.
Love is a dream where someone is dying, the faint
smell of shit and the memory of poems that breathe
for us each in this bed. I kiss you on the mouth
and I am crying, not just dreaming, not quite
certain, like when I would dream myself on the toilet
reading *Hagar the Horrible* and wake up
having peed the bed: The Wet Bed Dream.
The clock reads
seven-eleven. This I know because I opened
up my eyes, because I can.

Equinox

Now is the time of year when bees are wild
and eccentric. They fly fast and in cramped
loop-de-loops, dive-bomb clusters of conversants
in the bright, late-September out-of-doors.
I have found their dried husks in my clothes.

They are dervishes because they are dying,
one last sting, a warm place to squeeze
a drop of venom or of honey.
After the stroke we thought would be her last
my grandmother came back, reared back and slapped

a nurse across the face. Then she stood up,
walked outside, and lay down in the snow.
Two years later there is no other way
to say, we are waiting. She is silent, light
as an empty hive, and she is breathing.

At the Beach

Looking at the photograph is somehow not
unbearable: My friends, two dead, one low
on T-cells, his white T-shirt an X-ray
screen for the virus, which I imagine
as a single, swimming paisley, a sardine
with serrated fins and a neon spine.

I'm on a train, thinking about my friends
and watching two women talk in sign language.
I feel the energy and heft their talk
generates, the weight of their words in the air
the same heft as your presence in this picture,
boys, the volume of late summer air at the beach.

Did you tea-dance that day? Write poems
in the sunlight? Vamp with strangers? There is
sun under your skin like the gold Sula
found beneath Ajax's black. I calibrate
the weight of your beautiful bones, the weight
of your elbow, Melvin,

on Darrell's brown shoulder.

Tending

In the pull-out bed with my brother
  in my grandfather's Riverton apartment
my knees and ankles throbbed from growing,
  pulsing so hard they kept me awake –
or was it the Metro North train cars
  flying past the apartment, rocking the walls,
or was it the sound of apartment front doors
  as heavy as prison doors clanging shut?
Was the Black Nation whispering to me
  from the *Jet* magazines stacked on the floor, or
was it my brother's unfamiliar ions
  vibrating, humming in his easeful sleep?
Tomorrow, as always, Grandfather will rise
  to the Spanish-Town cock's crow deep in his head
and perform his usual ablutions,
  and prepare the apartment for the day,
and peel fruit for us, and prepare a hot meal
  that can take us anywhere, and onward.
Did sleep elude me because I could feel
  the heft of unuttered love in his tending
our small bodies, love a silent, mammoth thing
  that overwhelmed me, that kept me awake
as my growing bones did, growing larger
  than anything else I would know?

After

It wasn't as deep as I expected,
your grave, next to the grandmother who died
when I was three. I threw a flower in
and fizzled off the scene like carbonation.
My body of course remained but all else
was a cluster of tiny white bubbles
floating up, up, up, to an unseen top.

I wore your vicuna coat and an ill-
fitting cloche from Alexanders. I walked
among the rows, away from the men
covering the coffin, which was when I saw
'X', Malcolm, a few yards down, 'Paul Robeson',
then 'Judy Garland' then – the car was waiting
and we had to go.

                    The cocktail parties
must be something there! You'd discuss self-help
and the relative merits of Garvey-
ism with Malcolm. Robeson would read
in a corner. Judy, divine in black
clam-diggers, would throw back her head
and guffaw, smoke as many cigarettes
as she wanted.

                    Before you died I dreamed
of cocktail parties in your Harlem
apartment where you'd bring all our dead kin
back to life, for me! I was old enough
to drink with you, to wear a cocktail dress.
Like the best movies, the dream was black
and white, except for my grandmother's
lipstick, which was red.

from

THE VENUS HOTTENTOT

(1990)

The Venus Hottentot
(1825)

1 *Cuvier*

Science, science, science!
Everything is beautiful

blown up beneath my glass.
Colors dazzle insect wings.

A drop of water swirls
like marble. Ordinary

crumbs become stalactites
set in perfect angles

of geometry I'd thought
impossible. Few will

ever see what I see
through this microscope.

Cranial measurements
crowd my notebook pages,

and I am moving closer,
close to how these numbers

signify aspects of
national character.

Her genitalia
will float inside a labeled

pickling jar in the Musée
de l'Homme on a shelf

above Broca's brain:
'the Venus Hottentot'.

Elegant facts await me.
Small things in this world are mine.

2

There is unexpected sun today
in London, and the clouds that
most days sift into this cage
where I am working have dispersed.
I am a black cutout against
a captive blue sky, pivoting
nude so the paying audience
can view my naked buttocks.

I am called 'Venus Hottentot'.
I left Capetown with a promise
of revenue: half the profits
and my passage home: A boon!
Master's brother proposed the trip;
the magistrate granted me leave.
I would return to my family
a duchess, with watered-silk

dresses and money to grow food,
rouge and powders in glass pots,
silver scissors, a lorgnette,
voile and tulle instead of flax,
cerulean blue instead
of indigo. My brother would
devour sugar-studded non-
pareils, pale taffy, damask plums.

That was years ago. London's
circuses are florid and filthy,
swarming with cabbage-smelling
citizens who stare and query,
'Is it muscle? Bone? Or fat?'
My neighbor to the left is
The Sapient Pig, 'The Only
Scholar of His Race'. He plays

at cards, tells time and fortunes
by scraping his hooves. Behind
me is Prince Kar-mi, who arches
like a rubber tree and stares back

at the crowd from under the crook
of his knee. A professional
animal trainer shouts my cues.
There are singing mice here.

'The Ball of Duchess DuBarry':
In the engraving I lurch
toward the *belles dames*, mad-eyed, and
they swoon. Men in capes and pince-nez
shield them. Tassels dance at my hips.
In this newspaper lithograph
my buttocks are shown swollen
and luminous as a planet.

Monsieur Cuvier investigates
between my legs, poking, prodding,
sure of his hypothesis.
I half expect him to pull silk
scarves from inside me, paper poppies,
then a rabbit! He complains
at my scent and does not think
I comprehend, but I speak

English. I speak Dutch. I speak
a little French as well, and
languages Monsieur Cuvier
will never know have names.
Now I am bitter and now
I am sick. I eat brown bread,
drink rancid broth. I miss good sun,
miss Mother's *sadza*. My stomach

is frequently queasy from mutton
chops, pale potatoes, blood sausage.
I was certain that this would be
better than farm life. I am
the family entrepreneur!
But there are hours in every day
to conjure my imaginary
daughters, in banana skirts

and ostrich-feather fans.
Since my own genitals are public
I have made other parts private.
In my silence I possess
mouth, larynx, brain, in a single
gesture. I rub my hair
with lanolin, and pose in profile
like a painted Nubian

archer, imagining gold leaf
woven through my hair, and diamonds.
Observe the wordless Odalisque.
I have not forgotten my Khoisan
clicks. My flexible tongue
and healthy mouth bewilder
this man with his rotting teeth.
If he were to let me rise up

from this table, I'd spirit
his knives and cut out his black heart,
seal it with science fluid inside
a bell jar, place it on a low
shelf in a white man's museum
so the whole world could see
it was shriveled and hard,
geometric, deformed, unnatural.

West Indian Primer

(for Clifford L. Alexander, Sr., 1898–1989)

'On the road between Spanish Town
and Kingston,' my grandfather said,
'I was born.' His father a merchant,
Jewish, from Italy or Spain.

In the great earthquake the ground split
clean, and great-grandfather fell
in the fault with his goat. I don't know
how I got this tale and do not ask.

His black mother taught my grand-
father figures, fixed codfish cakes
and fried plantains, drilled cleanliness,
telling the truth, punctuality.

'There is no man more honest,'
my father says. Years later
I read that Jews passed through my
grandfather's birthplace frequently.

I know more about Toussaint
and Hispaniola than my own
Jamaica and my family tales.
I finger the stories like genie

lamps. I write this West Indian primer.

Ladders

Filene's department store
near nineteen fifty-three:
An Aunt Jemima floor
display. Red bandanna,

apron holding white rolls
of black fat fast against
the bubbling pancakes, bowls
and bowls of pale batter.

This is what Donna sees
across the 'Cookwares' floor,
and hears 'Donessa?' *Please,*
this can not be my aunt.

Father's long-gone sister,
nineteen fifty-three. 'Girl?'
Had they lost her, missed her?
This is not the question.

This must not be my aunt.
Jemima? Pays the rent.
Family mirrors haunt
their own reflections.

Ladders. Sisters. Nieces.
As soon a live Jemima
as a buck-eyed rhesus
monkey. Girl? Answer me.

House Party Sonnet: '66

Small, still. Fit through the banister slit.
Where did our love go? Where did our love go?
Scattered high heels and the carpet rolled back.
Where did our love go? Where did our love go?
My brother and I, tipping down from upstairs
Under the cover of 'Where Did Our Love Go?'
Cat-eyed Supremes wearing siren-green gowns.
Pink curls of laughter and hips when they shake
Shake a tambourine *where did our love go?*
Where did our love go? Where did our love go?
Stale chips next morning, shoes under the couch,
Smoke-smelling draperies, water-paled Scotch.
Matches, stray earrings to find and to keep –
Hum of invisible dancers asleep.

Nineteen

That summer in Culpeper, all there was to eat was white:
cauliflower, flounder, white sauce, white ice cream.
I snuck around with an older man who didn't tell me
he was married. I was the baby, drinking rum and Coke
while the men smoked reefer they'd stolen from the campers.
I tiptoed with my lover to poison-ivied fields, camp vans.
I never slept. Each fortnight I returned to the city,
black and dusty, with a garbage bag of dirty clothes.

At nineteen it was my first summer away from home.
His beard smelled musty. His eyes were black. 'The ladies love
my hair,'
he'd say, and like a fool I'd smile. He knew everything
about marijuana, how dry it had to be to burn,
how to crush it, sniff it, how to pick the seeds out. He said
he learned it all in Vietnam. He brought his son to visit
after one of his days off. I never imagined a mother.
'Can I steal a kiss?' he said, the first thick night in the field.

I asked and asked about Vietnam, how each scar felt,
what combat was like, how the jungle smelled. He listened
to a lot of Marvin Gaye, was all he said, and grabbed
between my legs. I'd creep to my cot before morning.
I'd eat that white food. This was before I understood
that nothing could be ruined in one stroke. A sudden
storm came hard one night; he bolted up inside the van.
'The rain sounded just like that,' he said, 'on the roofs there.'

Painting

(Frida Kahlo)

I've cropped the black hair Diego loves.
The swatches swarm about my feet.

I've cut a window in my forehead.
See? Diego, skull and bones,

magenta, nighttime fever-dreams.
His walls and walls of scenes of work,

brown women bare, female lilies.
I am spider-eyed among monkeys!

A year in bed   I still see blood
in crimson   olive   orchid   jade.

Look at my heart beat! See my veins!
As I lie bleeding in the street

a woman's sack of gold dust splits:
my bloody body gleaming gold –

I wish I could have painted it!
I will witness my own cremation
because ash is as lovely as fire.

Farewell to You

Each man on this slow train
has Bearden's Brueghel face,
his clean crown, putty-smooth,
eyes wise, no trace

of the colors, shapes behind them,
of paper cut to palms
or rump curves or half-moons,
or rooster-comb.

Through Newark, apple blossoms
line train tracks to the church,
and broken eyes of windows
as these cars lurch

past oil drums, blue and yellow,
like the blues singer's dress,
past empty boxcars stacked
like tenement windows,

or like piano keys
awaiting Fatha Hines,
Willie the Lion Smith.
Sound unwinds,

stanzas float in this notebook
at angles to the page
like the angles of music
in a Bearden clef.

Nausicaa makes jelly:
a green anemone,
snake-hips unmoored
in a blue-black sea.

These stanzas on the page
discarded strips from your collage
salvaged like America:
creole montage.

Honor the artist's vision
of a vast world, black and blue.
Beloved Romare Bearden:
Farewell to you.

Boston Year

My first week in Cambridge a car full of white boys
tried to run me off the road, and spit through the window,
open to ask directions. I was always asking directions
and always driving: to an Armenian market
in Watertown to buy figs and string cheese, apricots,
dark spices and olives from barrels, tubes of paste
with unreadable Arabic labels. I ate
stuffed grape leaves and watched my lips swell in the mirror.
The floors of my apartment would never come clean.
Whenever I saw other colored people
in bookshops, or museums, or cafeterias, I'd gasp,
smile shyly, but they'd disappear before I spoke.
What would I have said to them? Come with me? Take
me home? Are you my mother? No. I sat alone
in countless Chinese restaurants eating almond
cookies, sipping tea with spoons and spoons of sugar.
Popcorn and coffee was dinner. When I fainted
from migraine in the grocery store, a Portuguese
man above me mouthed: 'No breakfast.' He gave me
orange juice and chocolate bars. The color red
sprang into relief singing Wagner's *Walküre*.
Entire tribes gyrated and drummed in my head.
I learned the samba from a Brazilian man
so tiny, so festooned with glitter I was certain
that he slept inside a filigreed, Fabergé egg.
No one at the door: no salesmen, Mormons, meter
readers, exterminators, no Harriet Tubman,
no one. Red notes sounding in a grey trolley town.

A Poem for Nelson Mandela

Here where I live it is Sunday.
From my room I hear black
children playing between houses
and the El at a Sabbath rattle.
I smell barbecue from every direction
and hear black hands tolling church bells,
hear wind hissing through elm trees
through dry grasses

On a rooftop of a prison
in South Africa Nelson Mandela
tends garden and has a birthday,
as my Jamaican grandfather in Harlem, New York
raises tomatoes and turns ninety-one.
I have taken touch for granted: my grandfather's hands,
his shoulders, his pajamas which smell of vitamin pills.
I have taken a lover's touch for granted,
recall my lover's touch from this morning
as Mandela's wife pulls memories through years
and years

my life is black and filled with fortune.
Nelson Mandela is with me because I believe
in symbols; symbols bear power; symbols demand
power; and that is how a nation
follows a man who leads from prison
and cannot speak to them. Nelson Mandela
is with me because I am a black girl

who honors her elders, who loves
her grandfather, who is a black daughter
as Mandela's daughters are black
daughters. This is Philadelphia
and I see this Sunday clean.

from

THE BLACK INTERIOR

(2004)

from Preface

'Today as the news from Selma and Saigon / poisons the air like fallout,' wrote the poet Robert Hayden in the late 1960s, 'I come again to see / the serene great picture that I love.' In Hayden's poem, culture consoles and the artifact stands as a record of the human trace, a history of the individual voice and collective living spirit. Art is where and how we speak to each other in tongues audible when "official" language fails. It is not where we escape the world's ills but rather one place where we go to make sense of them.

Each day's news brings word of human atrocity and violation, as too many of us linger in pernicious and calcified ideas of who "the other" is. In desperate times when a citizen's raised voice seems to make no difference at all, it feels useful to turn again to the art and popular culture with which we speak, across difference, from each to each, to say, This is who I am, and thus, this is who we, collectively, are. What might we hope for and work toward?

Culture is one way I take in the world and venture beyond my boundaries, where I often find politics as well as aesthetic joy so deep I experience it in my body, where I shift and have sometimes shifted others through my own writing and teaching. The work I do is culture work, and culture is what calls many of us into the conundrums of the public sphere. Culture and politics need not present an either/or proposition if politics is restored to its original meaning – 'of the polis', the village, the community. Sometimes we encounter truths in culture not necessarily verifiable against census records or voting rolls. Sometimes in culture we find what we are hoping for before we have been able to articulate or enact it.

African American people are seen, imagined, and "known" through sociological and fantasy discourses, but the troves of our culture offer enlightening angles of vision. The historian laments caesuras in the historical record; the artist can offer deeply informed imagining that, while not empirically verifiable, offers one of the only routes we may have to imagine a past whose records have not been kept precious. The artist may, in fact, jog the historian to think in new ways about the data he or she might gather.

What unites these essays is an idea, a metaphor, of what I call 'the black interior', that is, black life and creativity behind the public face of stereotype and limited imagination. The black interior is a metaphysical space beyond the black public everyday toward power and wild imagination that black people ourselves know we possess but need to be reminded of. It is a space that black people ourselves have policed at various historical moments. Tapping into this black imaginary helps us envision what we are not meant to envision: complex black selves, real and enactable black power, rampant and unfetishised black beauty. What do we learn when we pause at sites of contradiction where black creativity complicates and resists what blackness is "supposed" to be? What in our culture speaks, sustains, and survives, post-nationalism, post-racial romance, into the unwritten black future we must imagine?

Toward the Black Interior

> I saw in Mobile a room in which there was an over-stuffed mohair living-room suite, an imitation mahogany bed and chifferobe, a console victrola. The walls were gaily papered with Sunday supplements of the *Mobile Register*. There were seven calendars and three wall pockets. One of them was decorated with a lace doily. The mantel-shelf was covered with a scarf of deep home-made lace, looped up with a huge bow of pink crêpe paper. Over the door was a huge lithograph showing the Treaty of Versailles being signed with a Waterman fountain pen. It was grotesque, yes. But it indicated the desire for beauty. And decorating a decoration, as in the case of the doily on the gaudy wall pocket, did not seem out of place to the hostess. The feeling back of such an act is that there can never be enough of beauty, let alone too much.
>
> ZORA NEALE HURSTON,
> 'Characteristics of Negro Expression'[1]

In my mother's living-room, there are shelves upon which she has arranged many beautiful and extraordinary objects. There is glassware shot through with cobalt streaks; a tiny, broken robin's egg; translucent, golden whelks; conch and limpet shells; dessert plates painstakingly painted as the peacock's splendid tail; wild branches of sun- and salt-bleached coral; sea fans dried in the course of their undulation; polished stones of all colors; and a dozen egg-shaped stones of different hues and sizes nesting in a Styrofoam egg carton. My mother calls them 'the shelves', the objects perhaps 'treasures'. I call the six shelves together an altar where her intuitive and artful arrangement divines power: the power of beauty itself; the power of precious objects put together to add up to more than their mere sum; the power of the stories behind each object; the power of a family and those who have blessed them and their home. Those shelves may be the presentation piece of the living-room and our family's home, but my mother alone arranged them; they speak of her aesthetic and her eye – an aesthetic made collective as it speaks for my family to announce that this is our home, sacred and beautiful. The living-room is where she reveals who we are.

Ntozake Shange writes: 'As black people we exist metaphorically and literally as the underside, the under-class. We are the unconscious of the entire Western world. If this is in fact true, then where do we go? Where are our dreams? Where is our pain? Where do we heal?'[2] If black people are the subconscious of the Western mind, where is 'the black subconscious', both individually and collectively articulated? My interest is not in psychotherapeutic culture and African American literature – though what a fascinating topic that is – but rather the marker such language offers for identifying complex and often unexplored interiority beyond the face of the social self. If black people in the mainstream imaginary exist as fixed properties deemed "real", what is possible in the space we might call surreal? Shange powerfully suggests that the contagion of racism seeps into the intimate realms of the subconscious and affects how black people ourselves see and imagine who we are. Indeed, by writing a book of dream poems I learned that race, gender, class, sexuality – our social identities – exist and have been "always already" constructed in the dream space, even when they are constructed outside of a racist impetus. I imagined that in dream space I was a somehow "neutral" self, but I found no such neutrality there. Yet social identity, in unfettered dream space, need not be seen as a constraint but rather as a way of imagining the racial self unfettered, racialised but not delimited. What I am calling dream space is to my mind the great hopeful space of African American creativity. Imagining a racial future in the black interior that we are constrained to imagine, outside of the parameters of how we are seen in this culture, is the zone where I am interested in African American creativity. 'The black interior' is not an inscrutable zone, nor colonial fantasy. Rather, I see it as inner space in which black artists have found selves that go far, far beyond the limited expectations and definitions of what black is, isn't, or should be.

As black people we have been bound by mainstream constructions of our "real", and we have bound ourselves with expectations that we counter those false realities. Problem Number One: The black body has been misrepresented, absented, distorted, rendered invisible, exaggerated, made monstrous in the Western visual imagination and in the world of art. The visual art world hegemony is very, very white. Black people have always made art and always imagined and understood ourselves to be other than monstrous stereotype. Therefore, the "real" black figure is a very different thing from the imagined one, and versions of what that "realness" looks like will frequently contradict each other. How do we understand "reality" when official narratives deny what our bodies know? Rape law before Emancipation classified black women as essentially 'un-rape-able' because black female bodies were usually somebody's property. Indeed, some men who raped black women were prosecuted as trespassers on another man's property. And some historians assert that not until the 1960s was a white man convicted of raping a black woman in the American South.[3] How does the body that has been raped assimilate that knowledge into a coherent narrative of self against the concomitant denial of what it knows?

Problem Number Two: The Negro is in vogue, and there is much clamor for his or her story. But how do we recognise if that story is "real", if it is "authentic:? Gwendolyn Brooks, in her heartbreaking poem, 'The Life of Lincoln West', writes of a little black boy about whom a white man says:

> THERE! That's the kind I've been wanting
> to show you! One of the best
> examples of the specie. Not like
> those diluted Negroes you see so much of on
> the streets these days, but the
> real thing.
> Black, ugly, and odd. You
> can see the savagery. The blunt
> blankness. That is the real
> thing. [4]

'The blunt blankness' is 'the real thing'; all other 'Negroes' are 'diluted' and therefore not 'real' enough. The white speaker looks at a child and can only see 'blunt blankness', which is what he reports to be real. And the black child is left to assimilate his inner sense of self with the knowledge that he has been, and will continue to be, so assessed by others.

We are too often prisoners of the real, trapped in fantasies of "Negro authenticity" that dictate the only way we truly exist for a mainstream audience is in their fantasies of our authentic-ness. Escaping from the compelling power of the imagery around us is no small feat. Where is our abstract space, our space of the real/not-real, our own unconscious? Is "real" the opposite of "abstract"? Of course not. But to take painting as an example, if African American work is in some way figurative (has bodies in it), it can pose a discomfiting challenge to the art world and to the black artist as well. Regardless of the artist's intent, he or she is painting against a history of deformation and annihilation of the black body and is thus challenged with resisting or redirecting the current (though ancient) vogue for a stereotypical black realism. Many black viewers are looking for "positive imagery", and while we often need those images, the power of the wish places constraints on what a black artist might feel free to envision and find in that subconscious space.

"Real" has found its place in black vernacular. Queer real, diva real, affirmation. 'You make me feel mighty real,' the late, great

Sylvester sang; and realness was the pinnacle of fulfilled existence, the most desirable state. Realness is also the ultimate litmus test that progress-minded black people place on one another, with often narrow definitions of how that realness might be embodied or enacted, or what it actually means to "keep it real". 'Got to be Real,' Cheryl Lynn wails, and her 'Real real real real real' repeats and careens and keens and becomes its own thing, the anthem of a generation, a call to arms, a call to each other and our newfound communal freedom-in-racial-and-sexual realness. The verb 'to be' becomes a new verb, 'to be-real'. In that disco-era hit, "realness" as sound has become abstract and therefore leaves room for invention and redefinition, a realness that goes so far as to be emptied of meaning and reclaimed as possibility.

The 2002 show *Black Romantic* at the Studio Museum in Harlem was subtitled, *The Figurative Impulse in Contemporary African American Art*. The show underscored a wide-ranging urge among diverse African Americans to see ourselves represented in art and to see fresh takes on that old sawhorse, "positive imagery". So many of these paintings feature uplifted heads, eyes, and chins, as though the black bodies attached to them are ever-striving, ever-hopeful, ever-expectant, ever-questing for the hope of a better racial tomorrow. As Valerie Cassel writes in the exhibition catalogue, 'Black Romanticism is still about the insistence of presence. The visual language used to render the images found within this exhibition is a vernacular that is easily consumed, yet rich in an art historical and collective history (albeit sometimes fictionalised). And, while sometimes pedantic, these images create a pragmatic space in which the black body is not only visible, but also safe.'[5]

In the spaces we designate and create, the self is made visible in the spaces we occupy, literal 'black interiors', the inside of homes that black people live in. Are the living-rooms of those homes, the spaces most consciously arranged and presented, representative of not only living space but of one's self, one's aesthetic self? Issues of public and private display are preeminent for African Americans. The living-room is a presentational space but at the same time, a private one. Within a home it is also a "not" space: not the bedroom, or the bathroom, or the kitchen, which is to say, the space where you do the things that are not done in those other spaces. Even in, let us say, one of the compact kitchenette studio apartments of Gwendolyn Brooks's poems, activity is nonetheless designated in certain spaces. If the "living-room" is not bound by walls, I am talking about the space where we don't do what we do in those other spaces, and the space of a home that is imagined as presentational. It is therefore a theatrical space, and, in a still visual realm, a space for tableau or *retablo*, with its connotations of the sacred. The living-room is where we see black imagination made visual, a private space that inevitably reverberates against the garish public images usually out of our control. What does how we arrange interior space say about how we live? And what does that say about who we are? Is there a particular power of the visual to make possible or imaginable that which is not the present reality?

In 1937, Benjamin Brawley, then professor of English at Howard University, wrote an extraordinary book called *The Negro Genius* in which he reviewed black cultural achievement through 1936. He wrote: 'The temperament of the American Negro is primarily lyrical, imaginative, subjective; and his genius has most frequently sought expression in some one of the arts.'[6] His argument would not stand up under the scrutiny of today's post-essentialism, or even the nationalism of a generation ago that eschewed notions of Negro naïveté or absence from the regions of the empirically intellectual, but this was nonetheless an important observation in its time for thinking about black genius. Brawley wrote:

> If one has taken note of the homes of Negro peasants in the South, he must have observed that the instinct for beauty insists upon an outlet. If no better picture is available, there will be a flaming advertisement on the walls. Few homes have not at least a rose-bush in the garden or a geranium on the windowsill.... In some of our communities Negroes are often known to "get happy" in church. It is never a sermon on the theory of the Atonement that awakens such ecstasy. Instead, this accompanies a vivid description of the beauties of heaven – the walls of jasper, the angels with palms in their hands, and, best of all, the feast of milk and honey. It is the sensuous appeal that is most effective. The untutored Negro is thrilled not so much by the moral as by the artistic and pictorial elements of religion.

The will to beauty, the will to fantasy, the will to wish, the power of wish, wish translated to action, all are identified and enacted through the power of the visual. The living-room is the space where this "takes place".

Contemporary artist Adia Millett makes child-sized dollhouses with very grown-up interiors that must be viewed by peeping in the doll-sized windows: Doritos, Crisco oil, and Pasta-Roni on the counter of the kitchenette, a plastic-covered couch, a shopping cart of miscellany, all the markers of specific homes and how their imaginary residents live, eat, sleep, and recreate, riffing on the fantasia of the dollhouse and the mass-marketed Barbie Dream House. Notably figureless, Millett's dollhouses make the act of looking inside explicit even as they control how much a spectator can see. You have to walk up to the dollhouse and approach it on its own terms, stoop and squint into the windows to take in detail after detail. Her work flips the script on questions of display. When we are not "public", with all that the word connotes for black people then how do we live and who are we? And how does this visual work make the move from public to private explicit?

Romare Bearden's totemic series, 'The Block', is a key work for thinking about the public display of African American private life. Bearden's 1971 collage, *The Block I*, is a long horizontal rectangle, setting up a sense of the forward movement of narrative from the start. Although Palmer Hayden and Archibald Motley could be called the artistic progenitors of the African American street scene, Bearden moved behind the façade of the block inside his subjects' homes and lives. For the buildings he has used plain brown paper, bricks he has painted himself, and what looks to be brick-patterned Contac paper, reminiscent of the wood-grain paper used by Picasso in his first collages. This block is bookended with a liquor store and a barbershop anchored in the center by the Sunrise Baptist Church. Bearden has painted the illusion of "cuts" into the buildings not solely in the regular spaces where windows would be but rather at random spots, as though cutting through the brick itself. In this way the viewer feels less like a Peeping Tom and more like a privileged observer placed squarely in the middle of life lived. The irregularity of the cuts adds to the element of spontaneity and therefore "authenticity". Yet Bearden also makes a viewer aware of this status of invasion, of looking in without having asked permission. Additionally, because we do not see into every room, the viewer is aware that choices have been made as to what to reveal and what to keep private. The grave boy looking out might be asking, Who are you? as the viewer asks the same question. The angels burst from the brick at the top of the work, making us aware of the constructed frame that defines and sometimes constricts a community as well as the spiritual necessity of imagining movement beyond those boundaries.

'The Block' speaks brilliantly to issues of secrets, privacy, life lived on the stoop, and the need to show and say more than stereotypes of Negro pathology. It calls to mind the act of coming into someone's home, invited or not; the collage makes you want desperately to see everything inside. Think of the extent to which black life is so consciously about presentation. Whether that image presented is church lady or thug, the sense that we are always being evaluated has everything to do with how we comport ourselves. Certainly this pull to respectability has been a tension at the center of our literature with different stakes: Frederick Douglass criticising Henry Box Brown for giving up too many details of how he escaped; Linda Brent whispering and pulling the veil over details of her sexual violation so the white ladies to whom she pleads her case could continue to breathe and hear her; Langston Hughes's early black critics urging him to keep a clerical job doing tedious data input for Carter G. Woodson rather than wait tables because office work was more respectable for an up-and-coming poet and then criticising his poems for drawing too heavily on the frankness of the blues tradition, et cetera.

When thinking about paintings of living-rooms by black artists as representative interior spaces, I interpret 'living-room' broadly, from the doilied table spaces of Horace Pippin's *The Thankful Poor* to the basement space of Palmer Hayden's *The Janitor Who Paints*, where the janitor's creative, intimate self is shown as he paints a portrait of a woman and her baby. The surprise of the painting is what it reveals, both about this space that might not have been thought of as anything other than a basement hole but is instead a light-filled site of creation, and about the janitor himself, known by the job he does cleaning up after other people and here illuminating another part of his inner self. Living-rooms are specific and revealing about class, as you see especially in the hard-working middle-class living-rooms where the few decorative objects are lovingly tended, where the room is a set piece, clearly used for occasion, and the occasion of the painting is a very particular remembering. These are on display in Kerry James Marshall's paintings of living-rooms with the glittered and winged dreams above revealing the interior wishes and tended hopes of the inhabitants who so decorously receive company.

In the Beauford Delaney painting, *Beauford Delaney's Loft*, bohemians hang out downtown in the not-Harlem, where realistic space and scale shift seamlessly. Real human figures become nudes who could be artist's models or works of art themselves. The real world and the made world – made and imagined as art-flow into each other in a realistic narrative of multihued groups of bohemians in a loft space. The open and high space of the loft distinguishes that New York domicile from the Harlem tenement. The surrealist moments where Delaney interrupts the realist logic of the painting allow us to experience the challenges to convention that is one of the raisons d'être of bohemian living.

More recently, in Pat Ward Williams's installation entitled *Move?*, a lamp, easy chair, and television mark the space as a living-room. But the literal writing on the walls of the installation, the rage on the walls, is the inhabitant's political unconscious made visible. The unguarded moments in paintings or poems where the aesthetic conventions break up or are destroyed, is, I think, the equivalent of subconscious revelation.

Gwendolyn Brooks's exquisite, terse early poems of the mid-1940s portray the interior living spaces of the "kitchenette apartments" of the black metropolis of Chicago's South Side and showcase the brilliant moves of a poet whose work in words evidences a keen understanding of the power of the visual, and the possibility of modernist interior representations to transcend the often-stereotypical portrayals of African Americans in public spaces. Brooks is a painterly poet of superb power of visual invocation whose work is in conversation with the above-mentioned painters of urban street scenes. In Brooks's artistic coming-of-age years in Chicago, fellow black artists, both visual and literary, on the South Side included Eldizier Cortor, Gordon Parks, Katherine Dunham, Charles White, Charles Sebree, Margaret Danner and Margaret Burroughs, among many others.

Brooks's work seems activated by something at first visual and unguarded, outside of the tangle of verbal representations of the people she wrote about. She is queen of the poetic tableau, and in her work we see the interplay between black life in public – usually in the specified space of the South Side of Chicago in the 1940s, full of migrants like her DeWitt Williams who was 'born in Alabama, bred in Illinois, nothing but a plain black boy' – and in startlingly intimate interior life.

Imagine a black Chicago that is finding itself the subject of the scrutiny of social science, from black social scientists St Clair Drake and Horace Cayton, with their landmark 1945 study *Black Metropolis*, and from many other white observers. Some strove to understand Bronzeville and its residents in their fulsome complexity, and others succumbed to the stereotypical imaginings that were the order of that day and this one with regard to black people in urban centers and the way they live. Black Chicago was understanding itself as a people seen; through the poet's eye, Brooks was able to get beyond the limitation of that stereotypical spectating.

The sonnet is a 'little room', and Brooks reveals the equivalent of painted tableaux in her sonnets. With 'kitchenette building', the poem that opens her first book, *A Street in Bronzeville*, the title names the general space, 'kitchenette building', and one can imagine she is daring her readers to conjure up what they know or think they know about those specific structures and their inhabitants. But as Romare Bearden moves us from the street and building fronts of his various 'The Block's to inside those individual houses, Brooks, too, gives us a poem that is a square window or doorway, a look suddenly in, and then deeply in, beyond 'garbage and fried potatoes ripening in the hall' to the 'white and violet' of dreams. In her epic 'Annie Allen', Brooks writes that the protagonist is led 'to a lowly room / Which she makes a chapel of.' She understands that any space can be sanctified, that space is what we have, and that if, as a poet, she makes space visible, manifest, then she is getting us closer to the inner lives of her poetic characters who tell us so much about black people in a very specific place and time.

Brooks is highly specific about interior space in 'The Sundays of Satin-Legs Smith', for example, where she takes us into the closet of an eminent fop:

> Let us proceed. Let us inspect, together
> With his meticulous and serious love,
> The innards of this closet. Which is a vault
> Whose glory is not diamonds, not pearls,
> Not silver plate with just enough dull shine.
> But wonder-suits in yellow and in wine,
> Sarcastic green and zebra-striped cobalt.[7]

The description goes on, and then the section concludes, 'People are so in need, in need of help. / People want so much that they do not know.' That portrait of an unlikely space, the closet, is a window into the subconscious life of Satin-Legs Smith. Indeed, in the stanza break after the description of the closet, Brooks tells us what she wants us to glean from the voyage in: 'People want so much that they do not know.' Yet she does not say, 'He wants so much', because it is more than Satin-Legs that this closet has revealed to us. The closet also represents the 'wants' and 'needs' of the women who turn to him, 'receptive', as the poem concludes, 'and absolute'.

Brooks's poem, 'of DeWitt Williams on his way to Lincoln Cemetery',[8] gives a sense of her acute awareness of the Afro-Modernist spaces of Bronzeville. Here DeWitt Williams, a 'plain black boy', migrant from the Deep South to the Windy City, dies young, and we follow his funeral procession down the specific streets of the South Side. The title 'of DeWitt Williams', suggests a Brooksian irony: this 'plain black boy' nonetheless is accorded the classically heroic pageant of a death procession and also accorded the formal title, 'of'. The Chicago singer Oscar Brown Jr sings the poem as 'Elegy', which unleashes a still-deeper understanding of the Afro-Modern aesthetics in the poem. 'Nothing but a plain black boy' is the refrain that sticks. The poem alludes to the spiritual 'Swing Low Sweet Chariot', but as Brown sings it, he invokes no tonal remnant of the original. Perhaps there is no heaven for DeWitt Williams. The repetition of 'sweet' in the line 'sweet sweet chariot' eliminates the full match of the spiritual reference and emphasises instead the sweet life DeWitt, and so many like him, loved and that took him down: sweet women, sweet wine, 'liquid joy'.

Brooks is getting at something more than mere irony in her last line, 'nothing but a plain black boy.' Nothing/but. Unbestowed and yet. You can hear the blues behind it, the deepest of blues. DeWitt Williams is 'born in Alabama, bred in Illinois', and Brown gives us a space, the musical blues space, for two beats after 'Alabama' and 'Illinois.' DeWitt is both sociological and specific, one of the multitudes who made the epic journey from the South to the South Side. The poem embodies and understands the blues beneath, and that seems to be quintessentially Afro-Modern, a fusion that brings together orderly, intricate European literary form, the blues's attempt to narrate the displaced collective in a single voice (when I sing I, they hear We), and the blues for what needs some blues sung.

As Brooks's characters move through spaces marked 'black', 'urban' and 'public', she gives us intimate details of what might be behind the millions of faces that have stared back at viewers for over fifty years. As painting makes the invisible literal, it can challenge African American writing to see what's underneath and inside the façades we have willingly and unwillingly worn. To SEE, to lay eyes on these 'black interiors', is at first startling. Then it is amazing.

NOTES

1. Zora Neale Hurston, 'Characteristics of Negro Expression', in *The Norton Anthology of African American Literature*, eds. Henry Louis Gates Jr and Nellie Y. McKay (New York: W.W. Norton, 1997), 1022.

2. Ntozake Shange, in *Moon-Marked and Touched by the Sun: Plays by African American Women*, ed. Sydne Mahone (New York: Theater Communications Group, 1994), 323.

3. See Adele Logan Alexander's comprehensive discussion of these issues,

'"She's No Lady, She's a Nigger": Abuses, Stereotypes, and Realities from the Middle Passage to Capitol (and Anita) Hill', in *Race, Gender, and Power in America: The Legacy of the Hill-Thomas Hearings*, eds. Anita Fave Hill and Emma Coleman Jordan (New York: Oxford University Press, 1995), 3-25.

4. Gwendolyn Brooks, *To Disembark* (Chicago: Third World Press, 1981), 27.

5. Valerie Cassel, 'Who Will Speak for Us: A Utopian Romance Novelette', in *Black Romantic: The Figurative Impulse in Contemporary African American Art* (New York: The Studio Museum in Harlem, 2002), 24.

6. Benjamin Brawley, *The Negro Genius: A New Appraisal of the Achievement of the American Negro in Literature and the Fine Arts* (New York: Dodd and Mead, 1937), 15.

7. Gwendolyn Brooks, *Blacks* (Chicago: Third World Press, 1987), 42.

8. Gwendolyn Brooks, *Blacks*, 39.

EU DECLARATION OF GPSR CONFORMITY

Books published by Bloodaxe Books are identified by the EAN/ISBN printed above our address on the copyright page. This digital reprint was manufactured by Lightning Source at the printing works indicated in their code. This declaration of conformity is issued under the sole responsibility of the publisher, the object of declaration being each individual book produced in conformity with the relevant EU harmonisation legislation with no known hazards or warnings, and is made on behalf of Bloodaxe Books Ltd on 28 December 2025 by Neil Astley, Managing Director, editor@bloodaxebooks.com.

www.ingramcontent.com/pod-product-compliance
Lightning Source LLC
Jackson TN
JSHW081616180426
101040JS00030B/578

* 9 7 8 1 8 5 2 2 4 7 3 0 0 *